DIGITAL M&A

MASTERY

Insights and Foresight for the

21st Century M&A Leader

By

Nitin Kumar

Contributing SMEs

*Vicky Fang, Nivedita Candade
and Cuneyt Buyukbezci*

DISCLAIMER

The contents of this book are not professional advice to guarantee success; the book is for educational purposes only. These observations, takeaways, and observations are based on my experiences with M&A in Management Consulting and Operating Executive Roles.

CONTENTS

Legal Notes

The publisher and the author are providing this book and its contents on an "as is" basis and make no representations or warranties of any kind about this book or its contents. In addition, the publisher and the author assume no responsibility for errors, inaccuracies, omissions, or any other inconsistencies herein. The content of this book is for informational purposes only and is not intended to diagnose, treat, cure, or prevent the commercial, operational, or financial position of a company or individual. This book is not intended as a substitute for the admission process of each Firm.

Using this book implies your acceptance of this disclaimer. The publisher and the author make no guarantees about the level of success you may experience by following the advice and strategies in this book, and you accept the risk that results will differ for everyone. The testimonials and examples provided in this book show exceptional results, which may not apply to the average reader, and are not intended to represent or guarantee you will achieve the same or similar results as the individuals or companies mentioned.

PREFACE

After spending several years in the M&A world globally, I published a few thoughts, experiences, insights and learnings over the years.

I have led hundreds of due diligences spanning Commercial, Operational, Technical, and Customer bodies of work. Led over 75 integrations and 25 divestiture separations, ranging from the small to the mega-deals. Having spent so many years in M&A, making many mistakes, observing behaviors, and delivering success. I have shared my thoughts on various forums like LinkedIn, Medium, Podcasts, and a variety of forums.

There was never any intent to write a book amalgamating the disjointed bodies of knowledge and thoughts, until some clients I served, my M&A network, friends, and people who have followed by blogs, soundbites, and other forms of social media urged me to do so.

Why? What did they think that I could do differently from being yet another book on the shelf?

These professionals felt that my articles often provided useful frameworks for understanding niche issues in the due diligence and M&A integration process where well-defined literature around those topics was not available. They thought these experiences could enhance their M&A thinking and deal execution.

There have been several books written on M&A, some of which have been best sellers and taught me the basics of integration in my early days too. The problem is that business has changed a lot over the last decade, but M&A has largely remained the same without adapting much, there are areas beyond the basics and these new scenarios but have no formal literature around them.

Many of my clients and M&A network has been frustrated with the lack of guidance in the "new" approaches to M&A or expansion of existing bodies of knowledge.

Encouraged by these comments and reactions from C-level executives, M&A integration leaders, business unit leaders, and other accomplished executives hungry for more topics, I spoke with them on what they would like to see under the so-called "lesser-known topics". During this process, I spoke to scores of executives, polled several through surveys, and used social me-dia to gather the areas in which these advanced topics were more sought.

In polling these executives, I was fascinated by the response that some issues were common between large companies, mid-market, and private equity firms, and hence wove some of my higher impact content together in this form.

The unified voice tacitly said that they all knew what the good ingredients of a "traditional" M&A were and largely knew the basics. Some, even though they might have a one-off gap in specific functional areas, for which they could get help externally. Some executives stated that they viewed the acquisition engine of their respective organizations as a core capability viewed as a competitive advantage. They were all grappling with the problem of how to take this capability to the next level and enhance their competitive advantage.

The results out coincided with my own belief there were several advanced topics out there requiring attention, however not everything was a common scenario. I used my experience and judgment to focus on a few topics that would make sense to consolidate.

My promise to readers

Today there are dozens of tools and analytical techniques applied to the M&A world, especially in M&A.

My promise is that I will not add to the existing clutter of literature or offer hope through this book. What I offer is a collection of small bite-sized nuggets of wisdom to shape your thinking, these are built on real-life experiences and tested in multiple deal scenarios. The content of this book reveals several niche areas in M&A and are problems that surface from time and again, they could help businesses increase their odds of success during the execution of deals.

The book is also meant for due diligence and post-merger integration pros who could catapult their knowledge to the next level by gearing themselves for the topics which will continue to surface at a greater frequency as M&A becomes more complex.

Next generation M&A

As the business world gets more complicated in the coming years, several of today's advanced topics will become common practices and the need to keep up and master these and emerging areas of M&A will keep you ahead.

Happy Reading and Happy Thinking!

Cheers,

Nitin Kumar

Chapter 1

THE DIGITAL M&A LANDSCAPE

The rules of business continue to be redefined by disruptive technologies, and at a global scale altering business models, value propositions, customer needs, interaction models, the economic logic for underlying profits, and the evolution of new, interconnected ecosystems.

The changes are more so in the last 3-4 years. There is disruption everywhere with technologies like Cloud, Software Defined Everything, Open Source, Artificial Intelligence, IoT, Blockchain and Augmented/Virtual Reality, etc. going mainstream and creating new business models across many industries. Older and more established players must reinvent themselves or be displaced into oblivion.

All this has changed the thinking behind how M&A strategy is conceptualized and executed i.e. integration. The very questions around the definition of value and how to maximize it has gone through a big shift e.g., what areas to focus on during due diligence? Which synergies does one focus on? How does one create value? etc.

Strategy is Hard, M&A Strategy is Harder

The Tech sector was the digital disruptor for the early part of this century and today it is also digitally disrupted. A lot of older and legacy technology companies missed the new paradigms and are seeking to acquire themselves out of the disrupted business models by acquiring newer technologies and enabling business models. The number of shifts in control points that companies must deal with is non-trivial today, the shifting controls are conflicting and hence make strategy definition and formulation a lot more difficult than prior years.

Some examples of these business model changing technology shifts are

- Hardware to Software

- License to Cloud

- Cloud to Edge

- Centralized to Decentralized.

- Decentralized to Centralized.

- Human to Machine

- Real to Virtual

- Voice to Data

- Data to Voice

- Closed to Open.
- Enterprise to Ecosystem

Which tech strategy to back? What is a winning business model? What to acquire? Where is the risk etc.? These are all tough questions to answer in today's dynamic and uncertain environment.

Impact on M&A Strategy and Due Diligence

All these shifts have affected the very thinking behind M&A strategy through integration, a quick look at the key changes:

- It is more challenging for companies to approach a new business model, as it is out of their traditional realm of doing business. For example, selling licensed software and SaaS have different economics, KPIs, and go-to-market approaches.

- Typically, the older (or new) model cannibalizes the new (or older) model making GTM decisions a lot harder.

- There are no conventional synergies to realize from back offices, life is all about product and revenue synergies.

- Disruptive technologies or capabilities are not just one thing, putting clear definitions on an array of required capabilities and their impact requires heavier alignment between corporate strategy and corporate development.

- Culture due diligence and Technology (not IT) diligence ascertaining source and sustainability of value become critical.

- Single acquisitions never materially transform business models, developing a view of assets in combination to foster a pipeline with an invigorated level of engagement with the target companies is more important than ever.

- Defensive vs Offensive plays need to be differentiated; the former is more dilutive.

Impact on Valuation

Traditional valuations on multiple EBITDA, DCF, etc. have broken down with valuations trending much higher making it harder to articulate this to boards and investors.

Many of my clients now feel that acquiring disruptive assets is expensive and harder to justify on valuation, value also means the direct impact on the equity profile or stock price. Markets would take better to an acquisition strategy that is cohesive and messages to acquisition leading to a higher value business model. In my experience we have four types of value-adding deals well received by markets:

- **Catalyst Transactions:** The first acquisition signaling acquirers intent to change and embark on embracing change and thinking about the future.

- **Strengthen the Stack:** Specific capabilities like AI. Cyber, analytics, etc., enhance the posture of the existing value chain and can lay the foundation for future acquisitions.

- **Creating Competitive Advantage:** Adding more capabilities across the stack to differentiate from competitors and be a disruptor in the future.

- **Attaining Scale:** Gain customer and market momentum at scale, displacing competitors, and future-proofing the acquirer for the near term while creating the runway for more game-changing acquisitions

Impact on M&A Integration

Ironically, the changing rules of business have not changed the mindset during integration. It is still hovering around two schools of thought i.e., leave the target alone or absorb it at the speed of light running the playbook from 2015 which does not scale to create value in 2025!

In my experience, the M&A integration process must undergo these shifts to adapt towards value creation:

M&A Integration Strategy

Scope M&A integrations are defined when specific products, customers, channels, and brands are added which differ from the current model, scale integrations are when similar products, customers, etc. are added to attain scale. All disruptive technology integrations are scope categories, but the integration degree may vary by the situations outlined below.

Level of Integration	Situation
No integration	No experience with acquiring disruptive technologies; The first deal to catalyze the transition to a new business model.
Limited integration	Scope integration rather than the scale integration i.e., investing where both companies benefit from the synergies.
Partial integration	Enhancing existing value chain in very specific areas, functions, processes, or value drivers; Be more surgical
Full integration	Experience with integration of multiple disruptive technologies; Major disruption to the existing business model while 'stimulating new capabilities

Figure 1: Integration Levels

Synergies

Traditionally companies have thought of synergies as cost or revenue only and approached it that way. Given there are typically no cost synergies (negative synergies due to underinvestment in back-office etc.) when acquiring smaller disruptive companies/technologies/business models, one needs to think about this differently. An approach I have frequently used is to look at synergies in three ways.

- Sequential synergies: If the acquirer (or target) does activity A, then the target (or acquirer) is now enabled to do activity B (sequential to A) previously impossible on the value chain.

- Reciprocal synergies: Acquirer brings X enabling Y for target and vice versa i.e., what can they both add to each other.

With this framework cost and revenue synergies are a byproduct, not a starting point, unlike traditional M&A integrations.

One other place to pay attention to is BETA synergies i.e., the collection of those reciprocal and sequential synergies that directly affect the equity profile or stock price. Isolate these value drivers upfront and track/measure/monitor/report them with more rigor while building them into the investor messaging.

Integration Management Office

Given the dynamics with integration, synergies, etc. there is an obvious impact on the IMO design and configuration.

- Lack of conventional synergies leads to the breakdown of the rigid functional configuration of the IMO, it is now all about having value driver being the workstreams as opposed to the functions. Gone are the days when six functional boxes were solid lined into an IMO!

- Many M&A professionals both within corporate, and professional services need to know separate value creation from just protecting value for Day One or focusing on the IMO process e.g., governance, reporting, tracking, playbook, checklists, etc. While the IMO can turn the cranks, provide structure, rigor, reporting, etc., and is still important It is the value driver work streams (and applicable functions) that create shareholder value when acquiring disruptive technologies or business models.

Leading Practices: From Experience and Industry Network

A lot of the transactions I have been part of and a few insights from my network in Silicon Valley revealed five success factors when acquiring disruptive and business model-changing technologies. The entire M&A continuum needs to adapt to the new world order, some insights:

- Building in-house capabilities on disruptive technologies and around targets in the acquisition pipeline

- Conduct rigorous Technology diligence and go across the stack and evaluate for scalability, stability, interoperability, security, extensibility, performance, etc.

- Proactively develop a range of new valuation models

- Develop proactive board, investor messaging and education during M&A strategy development; the initial set of transactions can be less accretive.

- Develop specific integration approaches, do not run the traditional playbook.

Chapter 2

UNDERSTANDING XaaS M&A

The Software-as-a-Service (SaaS) business model has revolutionized how companies consume and deliver software. Its subscription-based approach creates recurring revenue streams and many scaling opportunities. This chapter explores the intricacies of M&A due diligence and integration specific to SaaS businesses, providing insight into the unique aspects of SaaS that influence valuation, key metrics, and M&A integration challenges.

Understanding SaaS Business Models

Subscription and Freemium Models

SaaS businesses often operate on subscription-based models, where customers pay a recurring fee for access to the software. These models come in various forms, such as monthly or annual subscriptions, and can target individuals or enterprises. The subscription revenues generate a steady stream of cash flow and is higher quality of revenue than past incarnations of licensing and services revenues. A thorough understanding of the subscription model is critical during due diligence, as it directly affects customer lifetime value (LTV) and churn rates.

In addition to subscriptions, many SaaS companies offer freemium models. These let users access a free basic version of the software, with premium features available at a price. The freemium model aims to convert free users into paying customers. In M&A, the due diligence process must examine the conversion rates, cost of acquiring new customers (CAC), and the scalability of the freemium strategy.

Enterprise SaaS Models

Enterprise SaaS targets large organizations with complex needs, often requiring customization, integration with legacy systems, and dedicated customer support. Due diligence for enterprise SaaS focuses on long-term contracts, customer retention rates, and potential upsell opportunities. Understanding the buyer's industry and how well the SaaS product aligns with their specific needs is vital for assessing growth potential.

Implications for M&A Valuation

Understanding the type and depth of the SaaS business model helps in determining the company's valuation during an acquisition. Traditional valuation methods may not fully capture the future value of a SaaS business because of the importance of recurring revenue, scalability, and growth potential. Key factors influencing valuation include:

- Customer retention and churn rates

- Monthly Recurring Revenue (MRR) or Annual Recurring Revenue (ARR)

- Revenue growth rates

- Cost of Customer Acquisition (CAC) and Customer Lifetime Value (LTV)

During due diligence, potential acquirers must evaluate these metrics to determine if the company's value aligns with its growth projections.

Key Metrics for SaaS M&A

Traditional software businesses i.e., licensing models were very profitable and made money by selling licenses at high prices and then selling services and support at 90% margin or thereabouts. All the cash used to be collected upfront and life was great. With the advent of SaaS, one had to sell subscriptions and focus on customer life time value. The entire O2C (Order to Cash) process was reconfigured and metrics that mattered during M&A and valuation drivers changed drastically. A legacy company buying a SaaS (or XaaS business) had to undergo a paradigm shift while executing M&A due diligence, valuation and M&A integration. I will explain some concepts and metrics below.

ARR, MRR, and Churn

Two of the most critical metrics in SaaS are ARR (Annual Recurring Revenue) and MRR (Monthly Recurring Revenue). ARR and MRR provide insight into the company's predictable revenue streams and are important for forecasting future growth. Acquirers should thoroughly investigate both metrics to ensure they are stable and aligned with the company's growth goals.

Churn is another essential metric, reflecting the rate at which customers cancel their subscriptions. High churn can be an indicator of poor product-market fit or weak customer support. During due diligence, it is important to dissect churn metrics by customer segments to identify any red flags that may affect the long-term stability of the business.

LTV/CAC Ratio

The LTV/CAC ratio is a key indicator of the overall efficiency of a SaaS company's growth strategy. LTV (Customer Lifetime Value) represents the total revenue a company can expect from a customer over their lifetime. CAC (Customer Acquisition Cost) is the cost associated with acquiring that customer. A healthy LTV/CAC ratio is typically around 3:1, meaning the lifetime value of a customer should be three times the cost of acquiring them.

A SaaS business with a poor LTV/CAC ratio may struggle to generate sustainable profits. In M&A, it's important to look beyond just current revenue and investigate the company's ability to attract and retain customers profitably. This ratio plays a significant role in assessing the scalability of the SaaS business.

Revenue Expansion and Customer Upsell

Expansion revenue—revenue generated from existing customers through upselling or cross-selling—can be a major growth driver for SaaS companies. During due diligence, it's crucial to analyze the company's ability to upsell premium features, more licenses, or complementary products to existing customers. Expansion revenue demonstrates customer satisfaction and provides insight into potential future earnings.

M&A Integration in SaaS

The value drivers that create shareholder value in SaaS are numerous and complex compared to traditional models of software.

Managing Recurring Revenue Streams

One of the key advantages of SaaS businesses is their predictable revenue streams. However, managing these recurring revenues during the post-acquisition integration phase requires careful planning. Disruptions in billing cycles or subscription management can lead to customer dissatisfaction and increased churn.

The integration team should focus on continuity in subscription billing and customer support. Acquirers need to make sure the new ownership does not disrupt the customer experience. Any changes in pricing, service agreements, or product offerings must be communicated to customers to avoid confusion and potential cancellations.

Data Migration and Platform Integration

Merging two SaaS companies often requires significant data migration and platform integration. The technical teams must ensure a seamless transition of customer data, user accounts, and billing information from one platform to another. Poor data migration can result in lost data, disrupted service, and a diminished customer experience.

In a perpetual licensing model you O2C process is geared to accept and process all payment at once, where are XaaS brings payment processing at a set frequency as subscription. Integrating these systems will require rewiring of the back-office.

In addition, integrating customer relationship management (CRM) systems, payment gateways, and backend infrastructure must be meticulously planned to prevent operational downtime. The success of post-acquisition integration in SaaS depends largely on the efficiency of data migration and the smooth alignment of both companies' technical platforms.

Preserving Customer Experience and Retention

Customer retention is the cornerstone of a successful SaaS acquisition. Acquirers must make sure the integration process does not negatively affect the customer experience. This involves retaining key customer-facing staff, such as account managers and support teams, who have established relationships with the customer base.

The integration team should also focus on reducing disruptions to service availability. Regular communication with customers about any changes is essential to preserve trust. Providing a seamless user experience is critical for maintaining customer loyalty and reducing churn during the integration phase.

Strategic Considerations for SaaS M&A

Identifying Synergies and Cross-Sell Opportunities

One of the main drivers behind SaaS acquisitions is the potential to create synergies between the acquiring company and the target. Acquirers often look for ways to leverage the combined product offerings to cross-sell solutions to each company's existing customer base. Identifying synergies early in the due diligence process allows for a more strategic approach to post-acquisition growth.

For example, if the acquiring company offers complementary products or services, integrating them with the acquired SaaS platform could lead to significant cross-sell opportunities. These synergies increase customer value and provide more revenue streams for the combined business.

Technology Compatibility and Integration Roadmap

Assessing the compatibility of both companies' technology stacks is critical in SaaS M&A. Acquirers must evaluate the scalability and flexibility of the acquired SaaS platform to ensure it can integrate with their existing systems. This includes evaluating the architecture, programming languages, and cloud infrastructure used by the target company.

The development of a clear integration roadmap is essential to avoid potential technology bottlenecks. The roadmap should outline the timeline for merging both platforms, aligning development teams, and integrating new features. A well-planned integration roadmap makes sure technology integration does not hinder the long-term growth potential of the SaaS business.

Retaining Key Talent and Knowledge Transfer

In a SaaS acquisition, much of the value lies in the talent that developed and maintained the software. Retaining key personnel during and after the acquisition is critical to ensure a smooth transition and continued innovation. This is especially true for companies with highly specialized technical teams or strong customer relationships.

Knowledge transfer is another key consideration. The acquired team possesses invaluable insights into the product, customer needs, and future development opportunities. Acquirers should focus on the retention of critical talent and make clear plans for knowledge transfer to avoid disruptions in product development and customer support.

SaaS vs XaaS

What is XaaS?

"XaaS" is a collective term, which is called the delivery of Anything-as-a-Service. It recognizes a great range of products, tools, and technologies that vendors now deliver to users as a service over a network (usually through the internet) instead of providing locally or on-site within an enterprise.

There are many examples mentioned here to help you develop a better understanding. The most common examples of XaaS that encompass the three general cloud computing models are:

- Software-as-a-Service ("SaaS")
- Infrastructure-as-a-Service ("IaaS")
- Platform-as-a-Service ("PaaS")

SaaS provides many software applications to users ranging from Google Apps to Microsoft Office 365 to Salesforce. But PaaS's offerings like Amazon Web Services ("AWS"), Heroku, Elastic Beanstalk, Force.com, Google App Engine, and Apache Stratos typically provide preconfigured virtual machines ("VMs") and other resources for application development and testing. But IaaS lets the organizations deploy and configure the virtual machines hosted in a vendor's data center and manage those virtual machines remotely. Services offered by the IaaS include Google Compute Engine, Microsoft Azure, and AWS Elastic Compute Cloud. Some other examples of XaaS are:

- **Storage-as-a-Service ("SaaS"):** Provides data, application, and backup storage system in the cloud.

- **Database-as-a-Service ("DBaaS"):** Provides access through the cloud to a database platform. Public Cloud providers such as Azure and AWS have DBaaS offerings.

Many benefits and efficient practical ways contribute to the success and high grossing rate of

XaaS models. Most organizations prefer XaaS because the As-A-Service model can simplify the tangled chain of IT deployments and cut significant costs on operational tasks and expenditure. An organization finds a sense progress by freeing up Opex and resources. With every additional cloud service, an organization can shed pieces of its in-house IT infrastructure, thus leading to fewer servers, hard drives, network switches, software deployments, and more. Going to a more "asset lean" posture enhances overall organizational performance.

With less IT staff, an organization may experience less physical overhead (i.e., equipment space, power, and cooling). The decrease eventually leads to the downsizing of ad-hoc, temp IT staff and firefighting. It also gives the opportunity to the IT staff to focus on more important value-added projects for the business. As far as the consequences of outsourcing are concerned, the on-premises technology shifts many Capex ("Capital Expenses") to Opex ("Operational Expenses") for the business.

Anything-as-a-Service platforms continue to dominate cloud-based product solutions as processing and memory costs steadily decline and connectivity capabilities accelerate. The lower costs and higher efficiency associated with these services make them attractive to both the solution provider and the customer.

For solution providers, XaaS's offerings generate recurring and more predictable revenue streams than on-premises alternatives and typically enhance customer lifetime value. For customers, cloud-based solutions reduce upfront capital expenditure requirements, make cash outflows more predictable, and can be tailored for specific uses.

Unlike traditional M&A that relies on cost-saving synergies, transactions involving cloud-based service providers are mostly revenue-driven deals. They offer buyers the potential to scale up, close gaps in product portfolios, and become more deeply embedded with the clients by offering a wider array of customizable and/or integrated business solutions. On-premises solutions require extensive engineering, support, and professional services to maintain multiple legacy versions; meanwhile, these costs are exacerbated by the complexity of acquisition integrations. However, XaaS integration comes with its own unique considerations around deal execution, its impact on functional areas (e.g., marketing, sales, products, pricing, and customer service), and other related risks and opportunities.

Key Risks and Challenges During Integration of XaaS Acquisitions and Mitigation Plans

- When transitioning from a traditional on-premises business to a XaaS model, it is critical to educate the sales team on the new pricing model and how it differs from the on-premises model.

- Incentivize sales team to transition to a Xaas Model. Otherwise, two sales teams selling a similar product in different delivery mechanisms will cannibalize each other.

- Develop the new appropriate pricing model that meets the needs of your customers without creating internal conflict. Created a phased plan and ensure shareholders understand the reason for temporary revenue drops.

- The acquired company needs to leverage the in-place capabilities of the buyer — and they may need coaching on existing processes and infrastructure.

- Never underestimate the importance of integrating corporate cultures, culture is never right or wrong- it contextual. People must understand the change in their context.

- Sales culture differences and clashes can impede integration and impact revenue, add safety nets and interventions early.

- Integrating finance and operations should pose significant challenges than other in other deals. Changing cashflow and revenue recognition impacts all back-office functions.

- Sales cycles and quote-to-cash processes may differ among existing and acquired services, which leads to challenges for sales and finance teams.

- Customers should be able to try the XaaS product easily to decide on how the XaaS offering fits into the product suite and which version they prefer to use.

- Channel coordination (direct vs. indirect) of the XaaS offering is important for its success.

- Having multiple acquisitions spaced closely together makes integration efforts even more difficult.

- Make sure the M&A integration teams have representation across business units and operations teams.

- Bring all internal stakeholders to the table early. Sales and other functional areas should be part of the process. Engage the sales team and understand how they intend to go to the market. Learn from new product introduction practice.

- Put pilot programs into practice with select customers.

- Consider delaying integration efforts in areas where there is no immediate solution to integration challenges.

Concluding Thoughts

Identifying the right business that can complement or diversify a company's existing portfolio and drive revenue expansion is a major objective behind XaaS's acquisition considerations. To capitalize on the acquisition, integration must be carefully planned and executed.

Too often, companies rush into integration and destroy value in the transition process by addressing financial considerations before understanding the new product portfolio and determining what the sales teams need to do to successfully attract the customers. Branding, messaging, and operating models are afterthoughts since they rarely are focused on. A poorly executed strategy results in confused messaging, lack of organizational focus, and a likely loss of customers and synergy realization.

Depending on business model differences and the readiness for XaaS integration, it may make sense to leave the acquired entity separate during post-closing. While waiting for an opportunity for the integration, determine how product portfolios will be integrated and then build your business model through marketing and brand integration. By doing so, this will enable you to deliver integrated and cohesive messaging to XaaS and on-premises sides of the organization, your channel partners, and the customers. Once this is done, transition the sales teams, operating systems, and business processes

— only then you can lay the foundation to attract customers, achieve synergy targets, and realize deal goals.

Chapter 3

THE NUANCES OF PLATFORM M&A

Platforms are more than a buzzword. Seven out of ten of the largest global brands are platforms, and five of the largest international companies by size are also platforms with notable names like Microsoft, Apple, and Google among them. Data and facts both indicate platform scale is much larger than that of point products.

Platforms are two-sided marketplaces e.g., Facebook has users and advertisers, Uber has drivers and riders, Google has publishers and advertisers, etc. The more drivers, the more riders for Uber create a network effect at scale.

Mergers and acquisitions (M&A) have been a vital growth lever for products and platforms, yet the platform M&A, which is most valuable, is least understood.

Platform M&A is typically undertaken to add, enhance or multiply network effects. Typically, one side of the platform gets weaker over time and could require a boost through M&A rather than organic growth alone.

Product and Platform Differences

People misunderstand platforms as simply technical layers and glue. They might also not understand that "platforms" differ from "products," although they are often related.

A product is created, made or developed for sale or distribution. It can be a physical item, like a car or a piece of clothing, or it can be a service, like accounting or law. Products are typically designed to solve a specific problem or meet a specific need.

A platform is a type of infrastructure or foundation used to support the development, distribution or delivery of products. It can be a physical structure, like a stage or a desk, or it can be a digital environment, like a website or a mobile app. Platforms provide the tools, resources and support necessary for products to be created, marketed, transacted and sold.

A product and a platform, however, are closely related. A mobile app might be a product sold to users, while the app store or website which it is downloaded from is the platform that supports its distribution. However, a platform is something where the bulk of the value creation for the company happens outside of its internal functions (inversion) and creates two-sided network effects.

M&A Value Drivers

Strengthening one side of the platform, adding a new network effect, lowering the cost of platform operations, accelerating ecosystem reach, etc. are typical reasons to embark on a platform M&A.

M&As involving platforms can be complex and challenging because platforms often have unique features and dynamics that need to be considered. Some of the core value drivers for platform M&A include.

User Base

The size and composition of the platform's user base can be a key factor in determining its value and potential for growth. A platform with a large and engaged user base is likely to be more attractive to potential acquirers, because it provides a ready-made audience for new products and services. It strengthens any one or both sides of the platform, creating scale.

Network Effects

Platforms must show strong network effects, where the value of the platform increases as more people use it. This can create barriers to entry for new competitors and make it difficult for an acquired platform to keep its user base if the acquisition is perceived as unfavorable.

Openness

Openness refers to how much a platform, system, or environment is accessible and for others to use, change, or build upon. An open platform, for example, is one that lets developers create and distribute their own apps or services without having to seek permission or pay a fee. An open system lets users access and manipulate data or information without being restricted by proprietary technologies or formats.

Openness is a key value driver during M&A. The more you open the platform, the more adoption you get. However, it generates less direct revenue. One of the key aspects of M&A is about increasing openness to drive enhanced adoption and volume or reducing openness to drive high monetization. Integration can alter, enhance, protect, amplify, or change openness with a profound impact on the deal value making it a core value driver in Platform M&A.

Regulation

Platforms are often subject to various regulations, including antitrust laws, privacy rules, and consumer protection laws. These regulations can affect the feasibility and terms of a platform M&A and require careful consideration and compliance to protect value.

Inversion

The level of inversion is a key value driver, it indicates how much value is created outside the firm. For example, open innovation is the R&D, customer reviews are the marketing, etc. It affects the openness and operational costs of the platform.

Considerations for Platform M&A

- Acquire platforms for the right reason e.g., strengthen one side of the platform, add scale, increase inversion to reduce operational costs, or drive openness for scale. Usually, platforms acquire other platforms.

- Due diligence should evaluate all the core value drivers in addition to traditional diligence areas like commercial, financial, operational, legal, etc. Specific emphasis should be placed on the level of openness, inversion, and risks or opportunities created after the acquisition is consummated.

- Given all the functions are located outside the company, traditional functional M&A integration approaches do not work. IMO (integration management office) must be configured by value drivers as workstreams rather than functions.

- Synergies do not appear as cost or

revenue synergies but manifest themselves through network effects changing the KPIs from traditional deals.

- Speed to lower operational costs could break network effects, hence choosing the right speed to integrate is a must.

- The more the inversion and openness, the less the level of internal operational integration creates a departure from traditional playbooks.

Concluding Thoughts

Platform M&A has changed the way value is created, one must depart from functional M&A methods and think of value drivers.

The M&A integration process (day one planning or checklists, IMO processes, and synergy templates) are a given, they are separated from core value creation which requires strategy, operations, product, and platform skills to be contextualized as a part of M&A. Rigid playbooks from yesteryears have broken down as new paradigms evolve.

Chapter 4

ANALYZING NETWORK EFFECTS IN M&A

Introduction to Network Effects in M&A

As platform M&A unleashed a new era of valuations in the prior decade with deals like Facebook's acquisition of WhatsApp or Microsoft's acquisition of LinkedIn, the network effect was priced into their large valuations. These purchase prices significantly departed from the old economy metrics like multiples of EBITDA or multiples of ARR, etc.

Network effects refer to the increasing value of a product or service as more users participate, creating a self-reinforcing cycle that can significantly elevate a company's worth. For novices or old economy minds in M&A, comprehending these effects is important for informed strategic decision-making. The risks, opportunities, and values must be understood differently. This article aims to provide a clear, detailed understanding of network effects, leveraging examples to illustrate these principles in a due diligence context.

Understanding Network Effects

Network effects are central to many contemporary business models, particularly in the technology and digital platform sectors. The phenomenon describes how a product or service increases in value as more people use it, creating a positive feedback loop that can lead to rapid growth and increased market share.

Types of Network Effects

Network effects can manifest as direct, where the value directly scales with the number of users, seen in social networks like Facebook, or as indirect, where the value grows due to adding complementary goods or services, such as the Apple iOS ecosystem attracting a diverse range of app developers.

The M&A Context

In the M&A context, network effects can drastically influence a company's valuation and shape its strategic and operational growth potential. Overlooking or misunderstanding these effects can result in significant miscalculations, potentially leading to failed investments or missed.

opportunities. It is critical to understand the value and risk drivers in each deal. One must holistically evaluate network effects across multiple dimensions and through several lenses.

Evaluate Existence of Genuine Network Effects

Differentiating Real and Perceived Effects

There is a difference between standalone rapid user growth and network effect-driven growth. From an M&A due diligence perspective, it is important to understand what value each additional user is adding to the platform. Real network effects can be seen in Facebook's acquisition of WhatsApp, where each new user significantly increased the messaging platform's value, enhancing its utility and appeal.

Assessing Interaction Quality

The depth and engagement quality of user interactions are crucial. Platforms that focus on meaningful user engagement, such as Twitter's algorithm changes focusing on user interaction over mere growth, illustrate the importance of quality in network effects. If the interaction quality between users is sporadic or toxic, it will soon wither away, while executing M&A diligence one must focus on metrics like engagement rate, viral units, etc. rather than DAU (daily active users), or MAU (monthly active users), etc.

Examples

Investigating successful cases like Uber's strategic expansion into new urban territories can offer valuable lessons. Metrics such as user growth rate, engagement level, and retention rate are indispensable tools in evaluating the presence and robustness of network effects.

Scalability and Value in Network Effects

Assessing Scalability Potential

In M&A, evaluating the scalability of network effects is a key consideration. LinkedIn's evolution into a multifaceted professional networking and content platform showcases how network effects can be effectively scaled and diversified across different service offerings like professional networking, sales navigator, ad platforms, recruiting services, etc.

Identify Value Thresholds

Recognizing when network effects reach their peak in terms of value creation is critical. Netflix's investment in original content creation, catalyzed by a critical mass of subscribers, exemplifies identifying and capitalizing on the best point of value creation due to network effects.

Market Size and Expansion Potential

Understanding the potential market size and saturation point is fundamental in scalability assessments. WhatsApp's strategic decision to penetrate the Indian market, leveraging a vast and growing user base, highlights the importance of recognizing market potential when assessing network effects.

Defensibility of Network Effects

Strong and defensible network effects are competitive moats and form substantial barriers to entry. For example, Google's search engine, bolstered by its vast data accumulation and widespread user base, serves as an illustrative example of creating a formidable structural barrier through network effects.

Sustainability

The durability of network effects relies on continuous innovation and market adaptation. Amazon's foray into various market segments and its investment in emerging technologies like AI and smart home devices highlight how innovation can reinforce and expand network effects. These network effects are built on a base of strong users, buyers, and sellers, interacting with each other at massive scales, so much so that any business can be launched on the formidable and sustainable platform.

Legal and Regulatory Issues

Comprehending the legal and regulatory risks and opportunities is important in maintaining network effects. The regulatory challenges and antitrust investigations faced by companies like Facebook emphasize the complexities and potential legal hurdles in sustaining network effects. Understand data regulation, anti-trust rules, consumer rights, etc.

Diversity vs Homogeneity

Analyzing the relationship between user base diversity and the strength of network effects offers insightful revelations in M&A due diligence. A diverse user base coupled with strong network effects suggests a robust, inclusive platform, likely to have wide market appeal and resilience against market shifts. This ideal quadrant represents a company that not only attracts a varied demographic but also benefits from the rich interactions and cross-pollination of ideas and usage patterns.

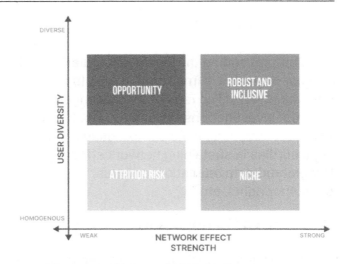

Figure 2: Network Effect Posture

But a homogeneous user base, even with strong network effects, might show a niche but potentially limited market reach. Such a company, while strong in its domain, might face challenges in expanding beyond its core audience. Assessing where a company falls within this matrix can reveal much about its market adaptability, potential for inclusive growth, and ability to innovate and appeal to a broader audience in an ever-diversifying global market.

Analyzing Viral Potential in Network Effects

Discerning the elements that contribute to viral growth is pivotal in an M&A due diligence process. TikTok's user engagement-based algorithm, which has propelled the platform's rapid growth, shows the impact of platform mechanics in driving viral network effects.

Juxtaposing Viral and Sustainable Growth

Balancing rapid, viral growth with sustainable long-term development is a nuanced part of network effects. Groupon's swift ascent and later difficulties highlight the risks associated with overemphasis on viral growth. One must separate sugar highs in a business versus the long-term viability of organic network effects.

Evaluate Social Proof and Engagement Strategies

Deploying strategies that use social proof and enhance user engagement can significantly augment a network's viral potential. Dropbox's innovative referral program, offering more storage for successful user referrals, is a testament to leveraging social proof effectively to stimulate network growth. Some metrics to deep dive into would be invites, referrals, incentive-induced virality, exposure virality, native viral feature, word-of-mouth effectiveness, etc.

Understand Core KPIs

Identifying the most relevant KPIs is crucial in assessing the health and potential of network effects. Uber's focus on metrics such as ride frequency and driver availability provide critical insights into the network's robustness, market penetration, and operational efficiency.

The "Take Rate" Factor

When evaluating companies with strong network effects, the concept of "take rates" is a key metric. Take rates refer to the percentage of the total transaction value that a platform retains as revenue. This metric is relevant in businesses where the platform acts as an intermediary in transactions between users, such as marketplaces, payment systems, or service platforms.

Take rates shed light on the value creation efficiency manifesting network effects.

Indicator of Monetization Efficiency

Take rates offer insight into how effectively a company monetizes its network. A higher take rate can show a strong value proposition and market control, suggesting that users will pay more for the benefits the network provides.

Impact on Network Health and Growth

The balance in setting take rates is crucial; rates that are too high may discourage user participation, while too low rates might not sustain business operations. The ideal take rate supports growth without deterring user engagement.

Finding the right balance between profitability and user base growth is a delicate task. Excessive focus on maximizing take rates can stifle network growth, while low rates might not be sustainable eventually.

Assess M&A Integration Risks and Opportunities

Post-acquisition, monitoring KPIs is essential to gauge the success of M&A integration. The acquisition of Whole Foods by Amazon, for example, can be evaluated using indicators like cross-selling rates, Prime membership growth, customer satisfaction scores, and in-store traffic patterns. There are also cost synergies embedded in the platform infrastructure, operations, and marketing. More on this in a separate article.

Security, Privacy, and Compliance

Ethical management, particularly in data handling and user privacy, has become a cornerstone of corporate responsibility in the digital age. The challenges faced by companies like Facebook in managing user data and privacy highlight the importance of ethical stewardship in network effects. Adapting to regulatory changes, such as implementing the GDPR in the European Union, or Uber's issues with labor laws underscores the need for companies to be agile and compliant in evolving regulatory environments.

Summarizing Key Questions

Asking the following questions during the due diligence process provides a view of the risks and opportunities around network effects in a target company's business model, important for making informed M&A decisions.

What is the Nature of Network Effects?

- Is the network effect direct (value increases with more users) or indirect (value increases due to complementary products/services)?

- How do these network effects contribute to the company's current market position?

How Strong are the Network Effects?

- What metrics or evidence indicate the strength and impact of the network effects on the company's value and growth?

What is the Quality of User Engagement?

- How engaged are the users? What metrics (engagement rate, viral units, etc.) support this?

- Are there any signs of diminishing user engagement or interaction quality?

How Scalable are the Network Effects?

- Can the network effects be scaled effectively across different markets or product lines?
- What challenges or barriers exist in scaling these network effects?

What is the Potential for Market Expansion?

- How large is the potential market, and what is the saturation point?
- Is there room for growth in new markets, and how might network effects aid in this expansion?

Are the Network Effects Defensible?

- How does the company protect its network effects from competitors or market changes?
- What legal or regulatory risks could affect the sustainability of these network effects?

What is the Balance Between Viral Growth and Sustainable Development?

- Is there evidence of viral growth, and how is this balanced with long-term sustainability?

- How does the company plan to maintain or grow its user base while ensuring sustainable business practices?

What is the Impact of Take Rates?

- How does the company's take rate compare with industry norms? Is it positioned advantageously against competitors?

- How does regulation impact take rates?

- If users derive asymmetric value from the network, does it support a higher take rate opportunity?

Concluding Thoughts

As digital M&A deals continue to rise, understanding the risks and opportunities in network effects is crucial for value creation. The existence of network effects, their scalability, defensibility, and virality are vital aspects during M&A due diligence. A comprehensive understanding of network effects can unlock substantial value by enabling more informed decisions driving successful M&A outcomes.

Chapter 5

M&A in the Artificial Intelligence Era

Artificial Intelligence (AI) has become a key driver of innovation across industries, enabling organizations to optimize operations, automate tasks, and leverage vast amounts of data for more intelligent decision-making. From healthcare, media, and finance to retail and logistics, AI is transforming business models and creating new growth opportunities. As AI technology evolves, mergers and acquisitions (M&A) involving AI-driven companies are becoming increasingly common. This chapter explores the critical aspects of AI M&A, focusing on due diligence, key valuation drivers, and integration challenges.

AI M&A

Artificial Intelligence transforms businesses through machine learning (ML), natural language processing (NLP), computer vision, generative AI, and other cutting-edge technologies. Companies are adopting AI to enhance decision-making, automate repetitive tasks, and extract insights and foresight from large datasets. As AI continues to permeate various sectors, M&A in AI is gaining momentum, enabling companies to acquire AI capabilities and leapfrog their competition.

However, AI businesses bring unique complexities to M&A transactions. These include evaluating AI models' proprietary nature, understanding data quality, and assessing the AI talent that powers these companies. As an M&A professional with extensive experience in the AI space, I have developed a framework for evaluating AI businesses that covers three critical dimensions: the AI technology itself, data assets, and the business model that underpins AI monetization.

AI Due Diligence

AI companies come in a variety of flavors e.g., some of the legacy big data folks now rebranding themselves as AI with highly optimized rules, but far from being cognitive or generative in their capabilities. These companies are also in various stages of the life cycle e.g., one having just the vision and talent, some have IP, others have a viable product, few have paid customers and a very limited universe of standalone AI start-ups have operating profit and scale. IP valuations can get contentious with proprietary technology and algorithms having no standard value measurements with patents enhancing value.

Founders and CEOs of AI companies know that they must focus their pitch on strategic valuation rather than traditional valuation drivers like sales, EBITDA, or even ARR multiples today. Most traditional acquirers and investors and wired for operational metrics-based valuation with AI or other disruptive technologies, this is breaking down today. The discounting methods do not hold today as AI companies are not willing to take a zero premium as many know their potential ability to accelerate the growth trajectory of acquirers, reduce costs, enhance customer experience, differentiate in the market, simply survive, or add vital capabilities for the future.

Talent valuation of acqui-hire transactions plays out differently on the value spectrum i.e., based on the technical credentials and track record of the personnel, level of cohesion, or tenure/history of working together. The industry thumb rule puts acqui-hires values are between $1 and 1.5m per employee, but AI companies go as high as $2.5m per employee (Source: Magister group research). Strategic acquirers must understand the market, the premiums and evaluate those against their strategic fit. The valuation rationale must also justify the IRR of an AI acqui-hire > 3x of organic hiring.

Conducting due diligence in AI M&A requires a deep understanding of the underlying technology, the data infrastructure, and the business model that supports AI solutions. My AI due diligence framework revolves around three essential elements:

1. AI Technology Assessment

2. Data Ownership and Quality

3. Business Model and Monetization Strategy

Let's explore each in greater detail.

AI Technology Assessment

AI is only as good as the algorithms and technology stack that power it. Assessing the AI technology during M&A due diligence requires a thorough understanding of the AI models in use, their scalability, and their alignment with the company's strategic goals. The following factors must be considered when evaluating AI technology:

Accuracy and Performance of AI Models

The performance of AI models is one of the most critical elements of AI M&A. Different AI applications require varying levels of accuracy. For instance, AI models used in autonomous driving need to have extremely high accuracy to avoid accidents, whereas recommendation engines may tolerate lower accuracy and latency. During due diligence, acquirers must evaluate the performance of AI models based on their accuracy, error rates, and predictive power. Benchmarks for accuracy should be analyzed relative to industry standards and competitors.

Scalability of AI Algorithms

One of the key differentiators of AI businesses is the scalability of their algorithms. AI models require vast amounts of data to improve over time through machine learning, which means that scalability is crucial for future growth. Acquirers must assess whether the AI models can handle increased data volumes and whether the computational infrastructure supports scaling. AI companies that have not yet solved scalability challenges may require significant investment post-acquisition.

Proprietary Nature of AI

Many AI companies differentiate themselves through proprietary algorithms or technologies. However, not all AI models are equally defensible. Due diligence should assess whether the AI technology is protected by patents or other intellectual property (IP) protections. Acquirers should evaluate the uniqueness of the algorithms and whether they offer a sustainable competitive advantage. Open-source models may be cheaper to implement but lack the same level of defensibility as proprietary AI technologies.

Data Ownership and Quality

AI models rely heavily on data for training and optimization. In AI M&A, the quality and ownership of data assets are as important as the AI technology itself. Without access to large, high-quality datasets, AI models lose their ability to learn and adapt to new conditions. During due diligence, acquirers must focus on the following key aspects of data:

Data Ownership and Access Rights

Data ownership is a critical issue in AI M&A, as AI models cannot function effectively without access to high-quality data. Acquirers must ensure that the target company has clear ownership or usage rights for the data it uses to train its AI models. Additionally, acquirers must verify whether the company complies with data privacy regulations such as GDPR or CCPA, which govern the collection and use of personal data.

Data Quality and Diversity

The quality and diversity of the data used to train AI models have a direct impact on the model's performance. Diverse datasets enable AI models to generalize better and avoid bias. In due diligence, acquirers must evaluate whether the data is clean, structured, and representative of the target market. Biased or incomplete datasets can result in flawed AI predictions, making data quality a key consideration for AI acquisitions.

Data Security, Privacy, and Compliance

Data security is another critical concern in AI M&A. AI companies that collect and process sensitive data, such as personal health information or financial data, must have strong data security protocols in place. Acquirers should assess the company's security infrastructure to prevent data breaches and ensure compliance with relevant regulations. Failing to secure data can lead to legal liabilities and reputational damage, which may erode the value of the acquisition.

Business Model and Monetization Strategy

AI companies typically monetize their technology through AI-as-a-Service (AIaaS), enterprise software, or AI-powered products. Understanding the business model is critical for assessing the long-term value of the acquisition. Key questions to address during due diligence include:

AI-as-a-Service (AIaaS)

AIaaS is a popular business model in which companies provide cloud-based AI services to customers. These services may include pre-built machine learning models, APIs for computer vision or NLP, and development platforms for building custom AI applications. When evaluating AIaaS businesses, acquirers must assess the scalability of the service, the subscription pricing model, and the platform's adoption rate among customers.

Enterprise AI Software

Many AI companies develop enterprise software solutions that are tailored to specific industries such as healthcare, finance, or logistics. These AI-driven products leverage machine learning to solve complex problems and optimize decision-making processes. Due diligence should examine the long-term contracts and recurring revenue streams generated by enterprise AI software, as well as customer retention rates and the scalability of the product.

AI-Enabled Products and Solutions

Some AI companies build proprietary products powered by AI, such as autonomous vehicles, AI-driven medical diagnostics tools, or recommendation engines. These products are highly specialized and require robust AI models. In M&A, it is important to evaluate the market demand for the product, the AI model's performance, and the potential for future expansion into new markets or verticals.

Key Metrics for AI M&A

To accurately value an AI company, acquirers must consider several key metrics that reflect the company's technology, data assets, and business model:

Accuracy and Error Rates

As mentioned earlier, the accuracy of AI models is a key indicator of their performance. Acquirers should request detailed reports on error rates, false positives, and prediction accuracy. These metrics can provide insight into the model's reliability and highlight areas where the AI may need improvement.

Customer Acquisition Cost (CAC) and Customer Lifetime Value (LTV)

AI companies, particularly those offering AIaaS or enterprise software, should be evaluated based on their ability to attract and retain customers. CAC and LTV are critical metrics for determining the profitability of the business. A healthy LTV/CAC ratio indicates that the company can acquire customers efficiently and generate long-term value from them.

Data Volume and Diversity

The size and diversity of the datasets used by the AI models are also important metrics. Larger datasets allow for more robust AI models, while diverse datasets help prevent bias. Acquirers should examine the data volume available to the target company and assess its quality and representativeness.

M&A Integration in AI

Integrating an AI company into a larger organization comes with its own set of challenges. Unlike traditional software companies, AI businesses rely heavily on continuous learning, large-scale data processing, and specialized talent. Successful post-acquisition integration of AI companies requires careful planning in the following areas:

Scaling AI Capabilities

AI models must continuously learn and adapt to remain effective. After acquiring an AI company, the primary goal is to scale its AI capabilities across the acquiring company's operations. This may involve increasing the computational power available for model training, expanding the data pipeline, and integrating AI models into existing products and services.

Retaining AI Talent

AI companies are often valued as much for their talent as for their technology. Machine learning engineers, data scientists, and AI researchers are critical for the continued development of AI models. Acquirers must develop strong retention strategies to ensure that key personnel remain with the company post-acquisition. Offering competitive compensation, equity, or other incentives can help retain AI talent and maintain the intellectual capital necessary for innovation.

Managing Ethical and Bias Concerns

AI models are prone to bias if they are trained on unrepresentative or incomplete datasets. Ethical concerns around AI, such as biased decision-making or privacy violations, must be managed during post-acquisition integration. Acquirers should establish governance frameworks to ensure that AI technologies are used responsibly and align with the company's ethical standards.

Redefining Value and Revenue Quality

Artificial intelligence is shifting business models from "Software as a Service" (SaaS) to "Service as Software," where AI does not just help with tasks but performs them, delivering direct outcomes. This shift redefines value delivery and challenges traditional metrics like annual recurring revenue (ARR). In this AI-driven landscape, tools become engines of actionable results, prompting startups and venture capitalists (VCs) to rethink what is high-quality revenue and how they evaluate potential.

From ARR to Outcome-Based Revenue Models

SaaS has relied on ARR as a stable, subscription-based income stream that supports predictable growth. AI changes this model by moving revenue from a subscription model to results-driven payments. AI companies charge for completed tasks, interactions, or specific outcomes, leading to revenue that varies with demand cycles and seasonal needs.

It introduces a new revenue— "annual repeat revenue," based on usage patterns rather than fixed access. The outcome-based revenue model requires fresh metrics that capture AI companies' real performance and align with their unique economics.

Key Metrics for AI-Driven Revenue Models

AI products differ fundamentally from SaaS, requiring updated metrics to gauge true performance, customer engagement, and profitability.

Deconstructing Revenue Components

AI revenue is tied to specific outcomes like tasks, interactions, or transactions, making it essential to analyze income at a granular level. This detailed view reveals demand fluctuations and identifies profitable areas, letting companies allocate resources effectively and adjust pricing models to optimize service delivery.

Trailing 12-Month Revenue Valuation

Given the volatility in outcome-based billing, ARR may not accurately reflect a company's health. Trailing 12-month revenue—or better, trailing 12-month margin—offers a realistic view of profitability, capturing seasonal demand cycles and variations in project needs. This metric lets founders and investors move from static revenue projections to evaluations that reflect actual market conditions.

Assessing Revenue Concentration Risks

In AI models, revenue often centers on high-usage customers, introducing risk if these key accounts reduce usage. AI companies must evaluate revenue concentration to understand their reliance on significant accounts, manage dependency risks, and build resilience against fluctuations in demand from major accounts.

Tracking Time to Value and Share of Wallet

Outcome-driven models benefit from tracking client metrics like "time to value" (how quickly customers begin generating revenue) and "share of wallet" (the part of customer spending captured by the AI product). Faster ramp times reflect effective onboarding, while a larger share of the wallet indicates strong market positioning. The combination of these metrics reveal growth potential and client engagement, which are essential for building sustainable, profitable relationships.

Activity Churn

In AI revenue models, "activity churn"—fluctuations or drops in customer usage—signals engagement and retention risks. Unlike traditional churn, it highlights early declines in product value, revealing potential gaps. AI companies can address usage issues, adjust offerings, and enhance client satisfaction, fostering stable, long-term revenue.

Service as a Software (SaaS Reconfigured)

Historically, full-stack, service-oriented models were seen as high-cost and hard to scale. But with AI, these models gain defensibility and scalability when delivering complete solutions with fewer resources and higher margins. AI-first companies that manage the full value chain can move beyond simply offering tools to deliver integrated, end-to-end value chains where AI is the primary driver, not a supportive add-on.

For example, an AI-driven real estate platform could manage listings, schedule virtual tours, and even handle negotiations. The approach bypasses the fragmented SaaS landscape by delivering a cohesive, fully integrated experience that strengthens defensibility and captures more value.

Reassessing Outcome-Oriented Models

This shift requires a reevaluation of what is "quality revenue." Traditional tech-enabled service businesses faced high operational costs and labor requirements, which deterred investors. AI changes this equation by replacing labor-intensive workflows with scalable, automated processes, enabling profitability with leaner teams. Today, launching another SaaS tool may struggle to stand out, while outcome-oriented, AI-first models gain traction by delivering unique, integrated solutions.

Real-World Examples of AI Pricing

Several companies have successfully implemented token-based and value-based pricing models. Here are a few notable examples:

•   Intercom's Fin: Charges $0.99 per resolved conversation, aligning pricing directly with successful outcomes.

•   OpenAI: Uses token-based pricing to charge for language model usage, adjusting token rates based on model complexity and resource consumption.

•   Midjourney: An AI image generator that charges $10 per month for about 200 image generations.

•   Grammarly: Evolved from a freemium model to a tiered subscription system, where advanced AI tools come with premium pricing.

•   Salesforce's Einstein Predictions: Charges $75 per user per month for AI-powered predictive analytics in sales, reflecting the direct value delivered to teams.

Strategic Considerations for AI M&A

AI M&A presents opportunities for synergies, particularly in industries where AI can optimize processes, automate tasks, or generate new revenue streams. Key strategic considerations include:

Identifying AI Use Cases Across the Organization

One of the primary advantages of acquiring AI technology is the ability to apply AI capabilities across the acquirer's operations. For example, AI can optimize supply chains, enhance customer service through chatbots, or predict consumer behavior. Identifying these synergies early in the M&A process allows for a more strategic approach to post-acquisition integration.

Ensuring Data Compatibility

AI companies rely on data to train and refine their models. Acquirers must ensure that the acquired company's data infrastructure is compatible with their own systems. This may require integrating data pipelines, building APIs, or developing new data governance processes. Ensuring seamless access to data post-acquisition is essential for scaling AI capabilities.

Aligning AI Development with Strategic Goals

Post-acquisition, the AI technology must be aligned with the acquirer's broader strategic goals. Whether the focus is on enhancing existing products or developing new AI-driven solutions, the integration team must work closely with AI product managers to ensure that resources are optimized for growth and cost savings. Acquirers should develop a clear AI roadmap that aligns with the company's long-term objectives.

Buyers must answer several key questions when looking at an AI asset.

Key questions and considerations (non-exhaustive list) to seek during AI due diligence and valuation would be:

- Is this truly AI or big data/other technologies layers with an AI wrapper (plenty of those out there)?

- Where is the value concentrated e.g., algorithm, specific part of the tech stack, background of people, team cohesion, vision of founders, etc.?

- Does the AI company bring in direct revenue enhancing speed to market, unlock additional insights, create a new market, augment existing products, and what does the revenue acceleration projection look like?

- Can the AI deliver on a scale? For example, are there limitations based on the data source, volume, structure, etc.?

- Does the AI company create cost efficiencies, productivity gains, and meaningful automation, and what part of those can add to the buyer EBITDA and what % can be passed onto the customers? What do those projections look like?

- How much boost does the existing analytics capability get? What is its timing and when does one feel the impact?

- How scalable is technology, what is the threshold of impact where it breaks down?

- What is the performance and how does it get affected by scale or change of environment?

- Is the technology stable, does all functionality work the way it is supposed to?

- What is the source and sustainability of competitive advantage? How replicable is it by others in the market?

- Does it have a risk of obsolescence?

- How extensible and interoperable is it?

- What are security features and how secure are they?

- Is there non-standard technology used, what is the impact on maintainability?

- Is the knowledge documented and well understood or is it tribal with few developers and architects?

- What is R&D processes, approval cycles, and investments in future features?

- Are there compliance risks?

- How much open source is used and what risks do they bring to the company?

- How does the acquired product, feature, or technology create synergy through integration?

- What is the strength of the management team, can they execute the next big vision and strategy?

Concluding Thoughts

M&A due diligence and integration in AI require a deep understanding of AI technology, data assets, and the business models that support AI-driven innovation. Acquirers must rigorously assess the performance of AI models, the quality and ownership of data, and the scalability of AI capabilities. Successful post-acquisition integration hinges on retaining AI talent, scaling AI models, and managing ethical concerns around bias.

AI will be embedded into everything we do; it will just be the new normal and a way of everyday life. The possibilities with AI are just limitless as it can open many new capabilities and new markets. The M&A race for AI has just begun and there will be a lot of M&A activity in the days to come.

Chapter 6

BLOCKCHAIN M&A

Blockchain technology has fundamentally transformed the way data is shared, and transactions are executed. Its decentralized, secure, and transparent nature presents unique opportunities for businesses across industries, from financial services to healthcare and supply chain management. Blockchain mergers and acquisitions (M&A) require a comprehensive understanding of the technology, the associated token economies, and the intricacies of decentralization. This chapter will explore M&A due diligence and integration in blockchain businesses, with a detailed focus on token-based models and how blockchain can drive value creation.

Blockchain M&A

Blockchain technology's potential reaches far beyond cryptocurrencies. It enables revolutionary business models by letting participants share and store data securely, without relying on a central authority. This shift could redefine industries such as finance, healthcare, event management, voting systems, and much more. Having worked extensively in the blockchain ecosystem, I have developed a framework for evaluating blockchain technologies and their business models from an M&A perspective.

Blockchain technology is built on chains of cryptographic blocks, each containing verified data. These blocks are interconnected, forming a blockchain—a decentralized ledger where all participants share and validate information. Blockchain technology provides transparency, immutability, and security by distributing control across a peer-to-peer (P2P) network.

Blockchain is being adopted in both open-source and closed-source applications. For example, open ledger systems like Bitcoin let anyone join and take part in the validation process, while closed or partially closed systems can be tailored for specific uses such as government initiatives or voting systems. The decentralization and transparency of blockchain have opened doors to new business models based on trust, immutability, and security.

As businesses increasingly turn to blockchain, M&A activity in this space has surged. The potential of decentralized applications (dApps), token-based models, and crypto assets requires careful consideration during M&A due diligence.

Blockchain Due Diligence

Due diligence in blockchain M&A is complex, given the innovative nature of blockchain technology. Evaluating a blockchain business requires more than just analyzing financials; it involves understanding decentralization, crypto assets, and the sustainability of the business model. Based on my experience, I use a three-part framework for blockchain due diligence:

1. Decentralization Test

2. Crypto-Asset Test

3. Business Model Test

Let's explore each in more detail.

Decentralization Test

Decentralization is the foundation of blockchain technology. By decentralizing data on a public ledger, blockchain makes sure no single entity has control over the system, which strengthens security and transparency. The more decentralized a network is, the harder it is for any one party to manipulate or alter the data. Blockchain can be decentralized across four key vectors: political, architectural, commercial, and contractual.

Political Decentralization

Political decentralization refers to how control is distributed among users or organizations. A blockchain becomes more politically decentralized as more participants engage in validating transactions and contributing to the network. In M&A, understanding the level of political decentralization is important, as networks with a few dominant participants may be more vulnerable to manipulation or central control.

Architectural Decentralization

Architectural decentralization refers to the underlying hardware and software that power the blockchain. In a decentralized system, no single computer or node controls the entire network. This reduces the risk of a single point of failure. M&A due diligence should examine whether the blockchain is truly decentralized or whether it relies on centralized infrastructure disguised as a decentralized solution.

Commercial Decentralization

Commercial decentralization examines the business models that arise from a decentralized network. In traditional financial systems, banks act as intermediaries for transactions. However, with blockchain, users can transfer value directly between one another, disrupting the traditional banking model. In evaluating a blockchain company, it is important to assess how the decentralized nature of the platform impacts its monetization and business logic.

Contractual Decentralization

Contractual decentralization refers to using smart contracts, self-executing agreements that operate on the blockchain. These contracts do not require human intervention once the terms are coded. Evaluating the smart contracts used in a blockchain platform is critical to understanding how transactions are automated and whether these contracts align with the acquiring company's goals.

In my experience, many companies that claim to be decentralized fail to meet these criteria. Only a small percentage of blockchain platforms truly achieve the level of decentralization that delivers value to users and businesses.

Crypto-Asset Test

Crypto assets are a key aspect of blockchain business models, providing the economic foundation for decentralized platforms. A crypto asset can be a commodity, token, or cryptocurrency. When evaluating blockchain companies, understanding the role of crypto assets is essential for assessing the potential for monetization and value creation.

Crypto Commodities

In the digital world, crypto commodities refer to the foundational elements that support blockchain platforms, such as computing power, network bandwidth, or storage capacity. These commodities provide the infrastructure necessary to create tokenized digital products. Popular examples include Ethereum and Cardano, which offer platforms for developing decentralized applications. When evaluating blockchain companies, understanding the scalability and utility of their crypto commodities is essential to determining growth potential.

Tokens

Tokens represent digital assets built on top of blockchain platforms. They can be used to access services, vote on governance decisions, or take part in decentralized networks. However, not all tokens have strong use cases or value propositions. During M&A due diligence, it's important to assess whether the tokens have genuine utility or are merely speculative. Some tokens may be valuable, while others are overhyped and offer limited value to the ecosystem.

Cryptocurrency

While there are many digital currencies Bitcoin remains the only true cryptocurrency with a proven value proposition as a decentralized currency. Bitcoin's role in blockchain and M&A is unique, given its widespread adoption and showed value. Other digital currencies may have potential, but many are far from achieving the same level of stability or real-world usage.

The value of crypto assets fluctuates based on market demand, regulatory changes, and platform adoption. So evaluating the sustainability of the token economy and its integration into the platform's business model is an important part of M&A due diligence.

Business Model Test

The final step in blockchain due diligence is evaluating the business model. Blockchain allows for the programmability of assets, trust, ownership, identity, and contracts (commonly called the ATOMIC properties of blockchain). The business model is built around how these properties are monetized, subsidized, and integrated into a sustainable value proposition.

Acquirers should assess whether the blockchain business generates revenue through decentralized trust mechanisms, token transactions, or smart contract automation. Understanding how blockchain technology improves the economics of the business, reduces friction in transactions, and offers new avenues for growth is critical for long-term success.

In my experience, a majority of blockchain companies fail either the decentralization test or the crypto-asset test. Of those that pass, about half still face significant challenges in building sustainable business models. Only a small percentage of blockchain businesses offer true long-term value, making rigorous due diligence essential for finding the best opportunities.

Key Metrics for Blockchain M&A

In addition to the decentralization and business model tests, there are several key metrics that acquirers must consider during blockchain M&A:

Network Security and Scalability

Security and scalability are central to the success of any blockchain platform. A blockchain that cannot scale to handle increased transaction volume or fails to secure its network is unlikely to achieve long-term success. Evaluating the technical infrastructure, consensus mechanisms, and security protocols is critical for determining the platform's ability to grow without compromising security.

Token Market Capitalization and Liquidity

The market capitalization and liquidity of tokens provide insight into the platform's economic health. High market cap and liquidity indicate a thriving token economy, but low liquidity may point to challenges in maintaining user interest or converting token holdings into real value.

Regulatory Compliance and Governance

Blockchain companies often face unique regulatory challenges. M&A due diligence must assess the target company's compliance with applicable laws, including anti-money laundering (AML) regulations and securities laws related to token issuance. Also, governance structures— whether decentralized or centralized—must align with the acquirer's risk tolerance and strategic goals.

M&A Integration in Blockchain

Integrating a blockchain company into a larger organization poses several unique challenges, especially when dealing with decentralized networks and token economies. Successful post-acquisition integration hinges on preserving the core elements of decentralization while aligning the acquired company's technology with the acquirer's broader business goals.

Integrating Blockchain Infrastructure

Blockchain infrastructure often operates independently of traditional IT systems. Integrating blockchain technology with existing systems may require significant development work, including building APIs or middleware to enable seamless communication between open-source decentralized networks and centralized infrastructure. Blockchain developers rarely work in corporations, operationalizing these integrations could require specialized skills or support from open course communities (if suitable).

Managing Token Economics and Governance

Token-based models present unique governance challenges. Token holders often have voting rights over platform decisions, which can limit the acquiring company's control. Acquirers must carefully manage token issuance, supply, and governance structures to avoid alienating the community while aligning the blockchain business with its strategic objectives.

Preserving Decentralization and Network Integrity

Acquirers must balance maintaining the decentralized nature of the blockchain platform and introducing the controls to manage risk. Making sure key network participants and developers remain engaged with the platform is essential for preserving the integrity and value of the blockchain.

Integrating blockchain infrastructure into a larger organization presents unique challenges compared to traditional software acquisitions. Blockchain networks rely on decentralized architecture and immutable ledgers, making it difficult to align with a company's existing centralized systems. Successful post-acquisition integration of blockchain requires:

- Smart Contract Management: Smart contracts automate transactions and execute business logic on the blockchain. Acquirers must make sure smart contracts are compatible with their own systems and align with legal requirements.

- Interoperability: Blockchain platforms must interact with the acquiring company's existing technology infrastructure, which may involve building APIs or developing middleware to enable seamless integration.

- Scalability: The blockchain network's ability to scale is critical for supporting growth. Acquirers should evaluate whether the infrastructure can handle an increased volume of transactions without compromising speed or security.

Implications for M&A Valuation

Valuation of blockchain companies is a complex process due to the decentralized nature of the technology and tokens as integral assets. Standard valuation methods may not accurately capture the potential of a blockchain business, especially where future adoption of the platform and token economy play a significant role in growth. Factors that heavily influence valuation include:

- Market capitalization of tokens

- Scalability of the blockchain network
- The level of decentralization and security of the technology
- Adoption rate of blockchain-based solutions and smart contracts

Token-based models add another layer of complexity. The volatility of token prices can have significant implications for the company's valuation. Acquirers must carefully evaluate the long-term viability of the token's use cases and market adoption trends to avoid overvaluing the target company based on speculative token prices.

Key Metrics for Blockchain M&A

Decentralization and Network Security

Decentralization is a cornerstone of blockchain technology, reducing reliance on a single point of control and distributing trust across a network of participants. For blockchain businesses, the level of decentralization plays a significant role in both valuation and risk assessment. Due diligence should evaluate:

- The number of active nodes on the network
- The consensus mechanism (e.g., Proof of Work, Proof of Stake)
- Security measures to prevent attacks, such as 51% attacks

- The governance structure of the blockchain and how decisions are made

Strong network security and decentralized governance are critical for the stability of the blockchain, especially when token holders or network participants play a role in decision-making processes. Acquirers must assess how these factors affect the blockchain's growth and resilience.

Token Metrics: Market Cap, Liquidity, and Utility

The tokens issued by blockchain companies can serve various functions, from helping with transactions to enabling governance. These metrics are key to evaluating the success of a token-based business model:

- Market Capitalization: The total value of tokens in circulation provides a rough measure of the platform's perceived value.

- Liquidity: High liquidity indicates a vibrant token market, letting users buy or sell tokens easily. Low liquidity could signal challenges for token holders who wish to exit the ecosystem.

- Utility: The primary function of the token, such as accessing services or enabling governance, is important for long-term adoption. A token with limited utility may fail to retain value eventually.

These metrics should be carefully examined during M&A due diligence to understand how well the token economy supports the business. The acquirer must also analyze the token's role in governance, as token holders may influence important decisions affecting the platform's future.

Compliance and Regulatory Considerations

Blockchain businesses often face unique regulatory challenges, especially when tokens are involved. Various jurisdictions may classify tokens differently, and regulatory compliance can vary dramatically across countries. The following are key areas to focus on during due diligence:

- Token Classification: Whether tokens are classified as utilities or securities impacts the regulatory framework.

- Data Privacy: Compliance with data protection regulations such as GDPR or CCPA is critical for blockchain companies that store or process personal data.

- Anti-Money Laundering (AML): Blockchain companies dealing with cryptocurrencies must follow AML laws and may be subject to stricter scrutiny from regulators.

Assessing compliance risks and understanding the regulatory landscape are essential for determining the target company's growth and avoiding costly legal complications.

Navigating Token Economics and Market Fluctuations

Token prices can be highly volatile, which presents risks for M&A deals involving blockchain companies. The value of a company may be closely tied to the value of its tokens, and sudden market fluctuations can erode value post-acquisition. Acquirers should develop strategies to manage token volatility, such as:

- Hedging Against Token Price Fluctuations: Using financial instruments to mitigate the risk of sudden token price changes.

- Managing Token Supply: Acquirers may need to manage the supply of tokens post-acquisition, either through buybacks or by controlling token issuance.

- Involving Token Holders in Strategic Decisions: Engaging token holders and aligning their interests with the acquirer's goals can reduce market volatility and foster long-term stability.

Concluding Thoughts

Blockchain M&A is a complex but rewarding process. By understanding the nuances of decentralization, evaluating token economies, and rigorously testing the sustainability of blockchain business models, acquirers can unlock the true potential of blockchain technology. Post-acquisition integration requires careful management of token governance, infrastructure, and decentralization, but when done effectively, it positions the combined business for long-term growth and innovation in a rapidly evolving decentralized world.

Chapter 7

IoT Driven M&A

The IoT M&A Landscape

The Internet of Things (IoT) landscape has significantly evolved since 2015, with notable changes in M&A activity. In 2023, IoT M&A continues to play a crucial role in corporate strategies, particularly in the tech sector. Recent reports indicate that the global IoT market was valued at $595.73 billion in 2023, with projections suggesting a growth to over $4 trillion by 2032, driven by advancements in AI, 5G, and cloud computing. This growing market has made IoT acquisitions highly attractive, especially in sectors like industrial IoT, connected devices, and analytics.

Source :(Fortune Business Insights)(PitchBook).

IoT M&A activity in 2024 highlights the increasing integration of AI with IoT, letting companies build smarter, more connected systems. Generative AI has emerged as a powerful tool in accelerating IoT adoption. Industrial IoT (IIoT) and connected services have been focal points, with startups leading the charge in providing cutting-edge analytics and hardware solutions. There were around 21,500 M&A deals across various sectors by mid-2023, with IoT continuing to attract significant interest

Source: (McKinsey & Company)(PitchBook).

Unlike the earlier years, where semiconductor transactions dominated, recent M&A deals have been more diversified. The focus has shifted toward software and services, which are expected to account for 60-85% of IoT-related spending. Companies are increasingly trying to acquire platforms and analytics capabilities, leveraging IoT data for new business models and revenue streams.

Applications and Services	End User Devices	
	Wearables	
	Software	
	Product as a Service	
	Emerging Services	
Data	Analytics	
	Data Publishing	
	Data Storage	
	Data Processing	
	Data Aggregation	
	Data Capture	IoT Security
Platforms	Proprietary Plays	
	Open Source	
	Middleware	
Connectivity	Network	
	Protocol	
	APIs	
Firmware	Edge Devices	
	Firmware	
Components	Microprocessor	
	Controllers	
	Signal/Radio	
	Components	
	Power	

Figure 3: The IoT stack

Traditional non-tech companies are also more involved in IoT acquisitions as they look to enhance their digital capabilities, contributing to 33% of total M&A values. High-tech firms continue to lead the charge with strategic acquisitions aimed at integrating IoT across verticals such as healthcare, agriculture, and smart cities.

This for IoT M&A turf underscores the long-term growth potential of the sector, with AI-driven innovation, scalability, and real-time analytics becoming central to its future.

Types of IoT M&A

Companies across industries are evaluating the impact of IoT within their landscape and identifying what capabilities they need to be competitive. As a result, many companies are investigating and exploring partnerships, consortiums, JVs, and M&A transactions – all of which require executive-level vision, a sound strategy, execution rigor, investment, and commitment. When it comes to IoT-centric M&A, there are six primary types that I have identified (outlined in the figure below).

Types	Focus	Description	Example(s)
Rapid Stack Expansion	Concurrent vertical and/or horizontal acquisitions	Performing acquisition in parallel to quickly solidify positioning and opportunities to play across the value chain	Google acquired DeepMind, NEST Labs, and Boston Dynamics
Stack Mobility	Vertical integration- moving up the stack	Extending capabilities to de-risk commoditization and create unique value propositions	CalAmp acquired Wireless Matrix; Amazon acquired 2lemetry
	Vertical integration- expanding down the stack	Enhancing Value Chain to reach new markets (industry verticals) or add capabilities to encahnce existing products and services	
Consolidation	Horizontal integration- expanding existing zone on the stack	scaling existing products or services into new verticals or customer segments	Digi International acquired Etherios
Defensive Plays	Consolidating Position	Merging to protect position in value chain de-risking scale and reach of larger players (smaller IoT firms)	Jawbone acquired BodyMedia
Preemptive strikes	Adding product capabilities	Enhancing existing offerings to accelerate use cases and keep competition from acquiring the capability	ARM acquired Sensinode; GE Worldtech Security Technology (2015)
Roll Ups	VC/PE firms buying platform companies	Buying mature, well-established players who can serve as roll up platforms, e.g., fleet management	Elliott Management Corporation investment in SIGFOX

Figure 4: The Types of IoT Deals

Characteristics of IoT M&A

While Consumer IoT focuses on delivering enhanced user experiences—such as fitness trackers, smart home systems, and wearable tech—Industrial IoT (IIoT) is driven by efficiency improvements, cost reduction, and leveraging data for better decision-making. Despite these differences, both consumer and industrial IoT players face critical strategic decisions: should they aim to own their ecosystems, provide the platform for an ecosystem, or operate within it?

Distinct Business Models and Drivers

Consumer IoT is often more experience-driven, targeting individual users with applications designed for personal convenience, health, or entertainment. For example, wearable devices and smart home systems focus on user-centric features like seamless connectivity, personalization, and user-friendly interfaces. Companies like Amazon, Google, and Apple have successfully integrated their IoT products into broader digital ecosystems by offering services that enhance the user experience, such as voice assistants, media streaming, and home automation.

But Industrial IoT aims at efficiency, automation, and data optimization. This sector leverages IoT for more robust, large-scale applications such as factory automation, supply chain optimization, and predictive maintenance. Companies in IIoT emphasize collecting and processing vast amounts of data to inform real-time decision-making, reduce operational downtime, and increase productivity. Industrial IoT solutions are more infrastructure-intensive and involve machine-to-machine (M2M) communication, integration with enterprise resource planning (ERP) systems, and enhanced security protocols.

Strategic Decisions in IoT M&A

One of the major challenges for companies in either IoT segment is determining their strategic role within the IoT ecosystem. Companies must decide whether they want to own the entire ecosystem (end-to-end control of devices, platforms, and services), provide the enabling platforms (infrastructure that other companies use to build and run IoT applications), or simply participate in existing ecosystems by offering hardware, software, or services that integrate with other platforms.

Companies are deciding to pursue different types of M&A transactions, in part, based on whether they have an open or closed technology stack.

Open technology stacks tend to attract thousands of third party developers and are attractive platforms for an IoT ecosystem.

In contrast, companies with closed technology stacks are more likely to internally develop product capabilities across all layers of the IoT stack.

Companies developing IoT platforms pursue vertical integrations to obtain the necessary product capabilities across different layers of the IoT technology stack.

Companies seeking to own or simply play in an IoT ecosystem tend to develop product capabilities internally and execute horizontal integrations when appropriate.

For technology companies, M&A in IoT is an opportunity to broaden capabilities across the stack. This typically involves acquiring expertise in key areas like:

- Data analytics and capture: Enabling deeper insights from connected devices.

- Device interface and management: Facilitating seamless interaction between IoT devices and platforms.

- Product design and contract manufacturing: Creating hardware that integrates with IoT services.

- Cloud integration and connectivity APIs: Ensuring IoT devices can connect to cloud services and operate efficiently.

Traditional tech giants like Google, Amazon, and Apple are moving into the hardware space, adding products such as Google Nest smart home devices or Amazon's Alexa-powered products to their established software ecosystems. These companies use M&A to integrate hardware and software, creating more seamless customer experiences while expanding their dominance in the IoT landscape.

Industrial Companies Moving Up the Stack

Industrial companies, meanwhile, are looking to move up the IoT stack to gain deeper control over data processing, analytics, and enterprise integration. Many are acquiring capabilities in:

- Device management and security: Critical for ensuring operational reliability and protection from cyber threats.

- Data processing and analytics: Turning raw data into actionable insights for improved decision-making.

- Business process intelligence and simulation: Using data to simulate different operational outcomes for improved efficiency.

For example, Siemens and General Electric (GE), both major players in industrial IoT, have acquired companies that provide AI-driven analytics and enterprise integration solutions. These acquisitions enable these companies to offer full-stack IoT solutions that encompass hardware and sophisticated data analytics capabilities and application enablement platforms.

Technological Advances Driving M&A

The demand for better data acquisition and management, low-power consumption, and connectivity is accelerating M&A activity in the IoT space. Emerging technological breakthroughs are critical in enabling next-gen IoT devices, such as embedded sensors, low-cost processors, and advanced software integrated with cloud platforms for real-time data analysis.

For example, companies are now prioritizing edge computing, where data is processed closer to the IoT device rather than in a centralized cloud. This reduces latency, enhances performance, and provides more immediate insights, particularly in industrial applications where downtime can be costly. 5G connectivity is also a key enabler, driving M&A activity as companies look to integrate faster, more reliable networks into their IoT offerings. The semiconductor industry, particularly in the development of chips tailored for IoT applications, remains a hotbed of M&A activity, with companies seeking to secure the latest innovations that will power the next wave of IoT devices.

Premium Valuations for IoT Targets

Strategic investors are often willing to pay premium valuations for IoT targets, especially those that can fill critical capability gaps in their value chains. Unlike traditional M&A, where revenue growth or cost-cutting may be primary drivers, IoT M&A focuses on acquiring strategic capabilities that enhance product offerings, improve data insights, or enable better platform integration. This shift in priorities reflects the understanding that IoT-driven growth is built on technological advantages and market positioning rather than short-term financial returns.

Companies are also increasingly pursuing multiple acquisitions in parallel to build out complete IoT ecosystems. This trend is especially pronounced in industrial sectors, where companies may acquire several firms across different layers of the IoT stack, such as device manufacturing, cloud connectivity, and data analytics.

M&A Activity Across the IoT Stack

IoT-centric M&A activity spans the entire IoT stack. Most IoT M&A volume occurs within Software and Apps/Services; however, larger deal values occur at the lower layers (Component and Hardware). The largest transactions have been horizontal integrations in the hardware layers by multinational companies targeting specific IoT technologies with a focus on consolidation within Industrial IoT (e.g. Smart Manufacturing).

The IoT landscape is dominated by application providers and we expect the IoT M&A trends of the past, to continue through 2020. Namely, higher levels of M&A volume at the software and service layers but higher transactions values at the hardware layers.

Given the high level of fragmentation at the software layers we expect future M&A activity will drive consolidation across these layers.

Stack Area	Select Aquisitions Across IoT Stack
Applications and Services	• Google acquired Nest Labs • PTC acquired Thingworx • Jawbone acquired BodyMedia • CalAmp acquired wireleess Matrix USA Inc.
Data	• Fidelity National Information Services acquired SunGard Data Systems • Digi International acquired Etherios • LogMein acquired Pachube
Platforms	• Amazon acquired 2lemetry • Huawei acquired Neul • Ericsson acquired Telenor Connexion's M2M Technology Platform
Connectivity	• Verizon Enterprise Solution Group acquired Hughes Telematics • Verizon acquired nPhase • Cypress acquired Broadcom's Wireless IoT Business including WICED.
Firmware	• Sony acquired Altair • Andreessen Horowitz acquired Samsara • Cisco acquired Jasper technologies
Components	• NXP acquired Freescale • Dialog Semiconductor acquired Atmel Corporation • Honeywell International Inc. acquired Elster Group GmbH **IoT Security** • GE acquired Wurldtech Security Technology

Executing the IoT M&A Strategy

Realizing Value from IoT M&A

At each layer of the stack, there are different synergy opportunities which can be mixed and must be taken into consideration by the acquiring company. Regardless of the type of acquisition and synergy strategy, companies should focus on retaining key individuals and performing cultural diligence early on to help identify risks with talent. Synergy focus areas include:

Revenue and Cost Optimization

At higher layers of the stack, where transaction values are lower, target companies have generally underinvested in IT and back-office functions. This characteristic constrains the value that can be achieved from cost synergies, therefore acquiring companies should focus on revenue synergies.

At lower levels of the stack, where acquisitions are larger in nature, there are often substantial cost synergies to capture. For example, NXP expects to achieve upwards of $200 million in costs synergies through it's merger with Freescale (according to company press releases).

User Integration

At higher layers, acquiring companies are more likely to pursue a user centric integration strategy where value is created through either acquiring additional users who create data, or through acquiring data that provides additional value to users. The focus is on leveraging content and data monetization to enable a variety of business models (e.g., advertising, subscriptions, cross-selling, up-selling).

Product / Platform Integration

Companies making acquisitions at both high and low layers of the stack, may consider choosing a product / platform centric integration strategy which focuses on creating opportunities for IoT platform development, product bundling, quickly rationalizing products or features, and identifying opportunities for new product development as a long term play. Bundles and pricing can drive a lot of incremental value if executed well.

Ecosystem Integration

Companies may also consider an ecosystem centric integration strategy, which emphasizes driving value through expanding product features and data analytics. A key aspect to delivering value is to make sure that customer segments, brand, products and pricing align very quickly to support the ecosystem.

Concluding Thoughts

IoT driven M&A requires careful consideration and isn't a guaranteed success. Risk factors include early adopter uncertainty, disruptive technologies, unclear or excessive valuation levels, and emerging partnership ecosystems / consortiums.. However, organizations with strong leadership and a commitment to IoT can successfully achieve their goals and realize healthy returns on their investments by optimizing synergy benefits. Given the expanding presence of connected devices , availability and value of data, and continual rapid improvements in technologies, IoT driven M&A should continue to play a large role within corporate growth strategies at both traditional high-tech companies and non-tech players.

Chapter 8

ANATOMY OF AN AQUIBOT DEAL

As mergers and acquisitions (M&A) evolve, businesses have adopted strategies to achieve digital transformation. A cornerstone of the transformation is to scale quicker, cheaper, and without adding costs of a human workforce. We are already seeing the advent of the algorithmic workforce with bots, digital humans, agents, algos, and holograms get integrated into workflows and drive value.

The traditional acqui-hire model, where companies acquire startups to secure specialized talent, has expanded beyond recruiting skilled workers. Now, M&A strategies are shifting toward acquiring cutting-edge technologies and digital capabilities, leading to the rise of acqui-bot deals. I recently worked with a SaaS company in transition to being an AI-first model and started a series of Acqi-bot deals.

In an acqui-bot transaction, companies are acquired primarily for their digital assets—such as bots, AI agents, machine learning models, algorithms, and even digital humans or holograms. However, this shift also brings new challenges, particularly in the areas of due diligence, valuation, and post-acquisition integration.

This chapter delves into the anatomy of an acqui-bot deal, offering a framework for navigating these new-age transactions. Let us examine the key considerations in due diligence, valuation, and M&A integration, and how companies can maximize the potential of these acquisitions while minimizing risks.

From Acqui-hire to Acqui-bot: The Evolution in M&A

Acqui-hire deals became popular in the tech industry as a fast-track method to secure specialized talent, especially engineers, product developers, and AI specialists. These deals primarily focus on human capital, allowing companies to onboard niche talent quickly to accelerate product development and gain market advantage. Many of these deals were based on the math of NPV of acqui-hiring bulk talent being greater than organic hiring. Typically these deals are originated by Business Units or Product Teams rather than traditional Corporate Development folks.

However, with the rise of AI, automation, digital experiences, algorithmic competitive advantages, etc., the focus of many acquisitions has shifted from people to digital assets.

In an acqui-bot deal, companies target technology rather than only talent. They try to acquire proprietary AI agents, machine learning algorithms, or other digital tools that automate tasks, enhance decision-making, or deliver new customer experiences. The shift presents new opportunities and adds new risks. Understanding the similarities and differences between acqui-hires and acqui-bot deals is essential for companies navigating this new terrain.

Similarities Between Acqui-hire and Acqui-bot

- Both are driven by the need to acquire critical capabilities (talent in acqui-hires, technology in acqui-bots).

- Both involve fast-moving transactions aimed at quickly addressing gaps in the acquiring company's operations or product lines.

- Both are often focused on small, innovative companies with niche expertise. Typically started by Business teams and hinges on NPV of hiring calculations.

Key Differences

- Acqui-hires focus on human capital, while acqui-bot deals focus on digital capabilities (AI, bots, agents, digital humans, holograms, etc.).

- Acqui-bot deals require deeper technological due diligence, particularly around the scalability and robustness of the acquired technology.

- In acqui-bot deals, M&A integration must address cultural alignment but also ensure the seamless integration of highly specialized digital assets into existing systems and workflows (or reconfigure them).

Key Considerations in Acqui-bot Deals

Acqui-bot deals come with their own set of unique challenges, particularly when evaluating and integrating advanced technologies. Here, we explore key considerations in due diligence, valuation, and M&A integration, with a focus on how companies can navigate these deals while maximizing value.

Due Diligence in Acqui-bot Deals

Due diligence in acqui-bot transactions is inherently more complex than in traditional M&A. Companies acquire highly specialized digital assets, such as AI agents, chatbots, and algorithms, which must be carefully evaluated for stability, scalability, security, interoperability, extensibility, performance, openness, and risks of obsolescence.

Focus on Context: Optimization vs. Adaptation

When an M&A deal occurs, the context of the business that AI previously operated in will undergo a shift and will need to adapt to its new operating reality. It must adapt to the acquirers systems, workflows, context, KPIsand not contaminate the existing baseline data set.

AI agents and bots are often optimized for specific use cases, customer bases, or industries. For example, an AI agent designed to enhance customer experiences in a bank with fast moving credit cards as the primary growth driver may be less effective when integrated with a bank where the primary growth driver is the large ticket home mortgage with lower pace.

- Optimization for Experience: Some bots and AI models are heavily optimized for delivering seamless user experiences within their original context. These assets may use tailored data inputs, user behaviors, and customer preferences that are specific to the company where they were developed.

- Optimization for Context: bots designed for highly regulated or specialized industries (e.g., financial services, healthcare) may be optimized for compliance, risk management, or operational efficiency.

When conducting due diligence, it's important to assess whether the acquired digital assets can be easily adapted to the acquiring company's context without losing effectiveness. Failing to account for contextual differences can lead to sub-optimal results post-integration, reducing the ROI of the deal or even driving up Opex.

Technology Scalability and Performance

Stability (minimal hallucinations), scalability, and interoperability are major factors in acqui-bot deals. Bots or AI agents that work effectively on a small scale may struggle when deployed across the larger infrastructure of the acquiring company. Due diligence should include stress-testing the technology to ensure it can handle higher volumes of data and transactions without performance degradation.

Key considerations include (non-exhaustive list)

- Data throughput: Can the AI agent or bot handle the data volume required by the acquirer's business?

- Cloud vs. on-premises: Is technology cloud-native, and does it integrate well with the acquirer's IT infrastructure? Can it scale as cloud-native or will it drive up Opex?

- Latency and speed: How does technology

perform under increased load, and can it meet the acquirer's speed requirements for real-time decision-making or customer interactions?

IP and Data Privacy

Another key consideration is making sure the acquired technology is proprietary and that there is no intellectual property (IP) or legal risks associated with it. The acquiring company must verify that the AI models, algorithms, or digital assets are owned outright by the target and that there are no licensing or third-party agreements that could create complications for post-acquisition.

AI models often rely on massive datasets to function effectively. Due diligence should confirm that all data used to train the models has been obtained legally and in compliance with privacy regulations like GDPR or HIPAA.

Valuation in Acqui-bot Deals

Valuing digital assets like AI models or bots is distinct from valuing traditional companies or even talent in an acqui-hire deal. Here are some of the key components of valuation in an acqui-bot transaction.

Proprietary Algorithms and Intellectual Property

The most valuable assets in an acqui-bot deal are typically the proprietary algorithms and models developed by the target company. These AI models may be capable of automating complex tasks, predicting market trends, or even interacting with customers autonomously.

The acquirer must assess the uniqueness of these algorithms (non-exhaustive list)

- How defensible is technology? Proprietary algorithms that offer a clear competitive advantage are highly valuable. However, if the technology can be easily replicated by competitors, its value goes down.

- How adaptable is the algorithm? Some algorithms are narrowly focused on solving a specific problem, while others are more flexible and can be applied across multiple use cases.

Valuing the Ecosystem

In addition to the technology itself, the broader ecosystem that the AI agents or bots operate within also plays a critical role in valuation. For example, an AI agent that thrives in a specific ecosystem—such as integrating seamlessly with an LLM system or working within a customer service chatbot network—may hold greater value than a standalone bot.

117

Understanding how the acquired assets will interact with the acquirer's existing tools and systems is essential. If the AI agents require significant retooling to function in a new ecosystem, their value may be lower.

Future-Proofing the Technology

In acqui-bot deals, the long-term viability of the technology is another important factor in valuation. Acquirers should evaluate how future-proof the technology is, considering :

- Is the technology at risk of becoming obsolete? Rapid advancements in AI and automation mean that some digital assets can quickly become outdated. The acquirer must assess the likelihood that the technology will need significant updates or overhauls soon.

- Can the technology evolve? Ideally, the AI agents or bots being acquired should be adaptable to future trends and advancements in AI. This means they should be modular, easily upgradable, and able to integrate with new tools or technologies as they emerge.

M&A Integration in Acqui-bot Deals

M&A Integration is often the most challenging phase of any M&A deal, and acqui-bot transactions are no exception. Successfully integrating AI agents, bots, and digital technologies requires careful planning, cross-functional collaboration, and a clear understanding of the technological landscape.

Fusing Technology with Context: Avoiding Sub-Optimal ROI

One of the most common challenges in acqui-bot deals is the contextual misalignment between the acquired technology and the acquirer's operations. For example, a bot designed to optimize user experience in e-commerce may not perform as effectively if repurposed for a B2B setting. Similarly, an AI agent designed for customer service in a tech company might struggle when applied to a regulated industry like healthcare or finance.

To avoid sub-optimal results, it's critical to assess the compatibility of the acquired digital assets with the acquirer's existing business model and processes. This includes:

- Adjusting the bot's algorithm to account for new data sets or user behaviors.

- Re-training AI models on different data to ensure they perform optimally in a new context.

- Reconfiguring systems to integrate seamlessly with existing digital workflows.

Managing Cultural and Process Alignment

Cultural alignment between teams is essential when acquiring talent through an acqui-bot deal. Digital engineers and data scientists who have developed cutting-edge technology may be used to fast-paced, agile work environments. Integrating them into a more traditional corporate structure could stifle their creativity and productivity.

Also, integrating bots and AI agents into existing processes requires alignment across departments. Often, the team that developed the bots might have run with rapid iterations and agile methodologies. This may contrast with the more structured, process-driven environment of a larger organization. The friction between these two approaches can lead to delays, miscommunication, or even failure in realizing the full potential of the acquired digital assets.

To manage cultural and process alignment effectively, consider:

- Maintain agility where needed: While the broader organization may follow structured processes, the newly acquired team developing and managing the bots or AI agents may need to retain some level of autonomy to keep innovating.

- Cross-functional integration teams: Create integration teams that include members from both the acquiring and acquired organizations. These teams should be tasked with harmonizing technical processes, fostering collaboration, and making sure the acquired digital assets align with the broader organizational goals.

- Phased integration: sometimes, immediate full-scale integration may not be the best approach. A phased integration lets the technology and teams acclimate slowly while maintaining their innovation capabilities.

Managing Change and Employee Experience

Another challenge in acqui-bot deals involves managing the experience of both the acquired employees and the existing workforce of the acquiring company. Unlike traditional M&A, where products, services, or talent are the primary focus, acqui-bot deals center on technology and integrating AI systems into broader business functions. This shift can create friction, particularly if existing employees perceive the bots and AI agents as replacements for their roles.

To address this:

- Transparent communication: Be clear about how the bots and AI agents will complement existing processes and employees, rather than replace them.

Outline how automation will free up time for employees to focus on higher-value tasks and drive strategic initiatives.

- Reskilling opportunities: Provide training programs for existing employees to interact with and manage the new AI agents or bots. Offering reskilling opportunities can enhance employee engagement and reduce resistance to the new technology.

- Incentivizing collaboration: Motivate teams to work together across both human and digital assets by recognizing and rewarding innovation that emerges from the synergy between human knowledge and AI-driven automation.

Bridging Digital and Human Talent: Contextual Alignment

While the focus of acqui-bot deals is on acquiring digital assets such as bots or AI agents, the human talent behind these technologies remains an essential element of success. Just as acqui-hire deals aim to bring in top-notch talent to enhance innovation and product development, acqui-bot deals often require the expertise of data scientists, AI engineers, and software developers who can continue to refine and improve the technology post-acquisition.

However, there is a potential disconnect between the digital assets being acquired and the human talent behind them. Digital assets like bots may be designed to optimize very specific business processes in their original context, and their creators often have deep insight into these processes. When the bots are transplanted into a new organization, their original creators are often best positioned to ensure they are adapted and integrated effectively.

Retention of key talent is critical in acqui-bot deals, but the challenge is not just retaining the talent—it's about ensuring this talent remains engaged and empowered to continue innovating. Here are considerations to bridge the gap between the digital assets and the human teams:

- Ownership of digital transformation: Empower the acquired AI engineers and data scientists to lead digital transformation efforts within the acquiring company. By giving them ownership of key projects and decisions, they can help optimize the integration of the bots and AI agents.

- Innovation labs: Consider establishing innovation labs or centers of excellence where the acquired team can continue developing new AI models or bots. This lets the acquired talent focus on their core competencies while remaining aligned with the overall business strategy.

- Clear role definition: Ensure that the roles of the acquired talent are clearly defined and integrated into the organizational structure of the acquirer. Ambiguity around roles and responsibilities can lead to frustration and ultimately higher attrition rates.

Measuring Success in Acqui-bot Deals

Measuring the success of an acqui-bot transaction goes beyond traditional M&A metrics such as cost synergies or revenue growth. Given these deals, specific metrics around technology performance and strategic alignment become critical. Here are some key performance indicators (KPIs) that can be used to evaluate the success of an acqui-bot deal:

Time to Market for AI-Enhanced Products

One of the primary goals of an acqui-bot deal is to bring innovative AI-driven products or processes to market faster. So time to market is an important metric. This includes tracking how quickly the acquired technology can be adapted, integrated, and scaled within the acquirer's existing product or service offerings.

ROI from Digital Assets

Return on investment (ROI) for digital assets such as AI agents, bots, or algorithms should be calculated based on their ability to reduce operational costs, improve customer experiences, or increase efficiency. This could include metrics such as:

- Cost savings from automation: How much are the bots or AI agents saving by automating routine tasks?

- Revenue growth from AI-enhanced products: Are the new AI-driven products creating additional revenue streams?

- Customer experience improvements: How has the customer experience improved through digital agents or AI chatbots?

Employee Engagement and Skill Transfer

Often, the acquired technology requires integration with existing processes and teams. Measuring how effectively the acquired talent is transferring their knowledge and skills to the broader organization can be an important success factor. Employee engagement scores, retention rates of acquired talent, and knowledge transfer metrics can provide insights into how well the teams are integrating.

The Future of Acqui-bot Deals: Opportunities and Risks

As businesses increasingly rely on AI and automation to drive growth, acqui-bot deals are poised to become a standard part of the M&A landscape. However, the success of these deals will depend on how well acquirers manage the complexities of integrating cutting-edge digital assets into their existing operations.

Opportunities

- Rapid digital transformation: Acqui-bot deals offer companies a way to quickly embrace digital transformation by acquiring AI agents and bots already optimized for specific business functions.

- New revenue streams: AI-enhanced products and services have the potential to create new revenue streams, particularly in industries such as healthcare, finance, retail, and customer service.

- Operational efficiencies: Bots and AI agents can automate routine tasks, letting human employees focus on higher-value work and improving overall productivity.

Risks

- Contextual misalignment: AI agents or bots optimized for one company's processes may not perform as effectively when transplanted into a different business environment. Acquirers must carefully assess how adaptable the technology is before making the deal.

- Talent retention: Retaining key AI engineers and developers is essential to making sure the acquired technology continues to evolve and improve. Without proper retention strategies, the acquiring company risks losing the talent that makes the technology valuable.

- Integration complexity: Integrating digital assets such as AI models or bots into existing IT infrastructure can be technically challenging, particularly if the acquirer's legacy systems are not designed to handle advanced AI technologies.

Concluding Thoughts

Acqui-bot deals represent the next frontier in M&A, as companies increasingly try to acquire talent and the digital assets that can drive their growth. However, these transactions come with unique challenges, particularly when adapting AI agents, bots, and digital capabilities to a new business context.

Successful acqui-bot deals require a thorough due diligence process, a nuanced approach to valuation, and a well-thought-out IRR calculation and a new M&A integration execution approach.

Chapter 9

Driving Synergies from APIs

Application Programming Interfaces (APIs) have become essential to the digital economy, facilitating the integration and communication of different systems, platforms, and services. APIs give businesses the capability to scale operations, innovate quickly, and drive synergies, particularly during mergers and acquisitions (M&A). By connecting various software systems, APIs offer flexibility and agility, which is important in the post-acquisition phase when companies are trying to integrate and maximize value.

The rise of APIs has changed the way companies think about software, ecosystems, and revenue generation. APIs let companies build, extend, and monetize their systems more efficiently by enabling interconnectivity between disparate platforms. For organizations involved in M&A, APIs are becoming a critical factor in accelerating post-merger integration, capturing synergies, and unlocking new revenue streams.

Historically, M&A focused on synergies in terms of cost savings or scaling operations. Today, however, the focus has shifted to revenue synergies and the ability to innovate through technology, with APIs playing a pivotal role. Companies acquiring others in the tech space, or traditional companies transitioning to tech-centric models, use APIs to rapidly integrate and unlock value from newly acquired assets. APIs also let acquirers tap into external ecosystems and enhance their platforms with third-party services.

This chapter explores how APIs can drive synergies in M&A by streamlining due diligence, influencing valuation, and helping with post-acquisition integration. In an era where "software-defined everything" dominates business models, APIs offer companies the ability to quickly monetize ecosystems, drive innovation, and expand capabilities across both internal and external channels.

Categorizing APIs

To fully leverage the power of APIs during M&A, it is important to understand the different types of APIs and their strategic roles within an organization. Broadly speaking, APIs can be categorized into Internal, Partner, and Open APIs, each serving a different purpose in driving synergies.

Internal APIs

Internal APIs are used within an organization to integrate internal systems and streamline operations. These APIs provide the infrastructure that connects departments, services, and platforms, allowing for seamless data flow and process automation. In M&A, internal APIs are critical for merging operational workflows, aligning systems, and ensuring business continuity.

For example, when Company A acquires Company B, internal APIs let the two companies integrate their respective Customer Relationship Management (CRM) systems or Enterprise Resource Planning (ERP) systems without having to completely overhaul their technology stack.

Partner APIs

Partner APIs are designed for integration with external business partners. These APIs help with collaboration, allow for data sharing, and enable companies to offer enhanced services to customers by tapping into third-party solutions. During M&A, partner APIs are valuable in expanding market reach and enabling access to new ecosystems.

For example, a financial services company acquiring a fintech firm may use partner APIs to integrate third-party payment services, enabling customers to perform new types of transactions seamlessly.

Open APIs

Open APIs, also known as public APIs, are available to external developers and third-party providers. They let external parties build applications or services that integrate with the company's platform. Open APIs enable the development of new products, create a developer community, and help companies expand their ecosystem by connecting to new markets.

In M&A, open APIs can be a main cause of innovation. For example, a social media platform acquiring an AI-based analytics firm can leverage open APIs to let third-party developers build new tools that enhance user engagement.

Risks and Opportunities with APIs in M&A

APIs offer tremendous potential for driving synergies in mergers and acquisitions, but they also come with inherent risks. Understanding these risks while recognizing the opportunities that APIs present is important for achieving a successful integration and maximizing value post-acquisition. This section examines both the risks and opportunities associated with APIs in M&A transactions.

Risks of APIs in M&A

- Security Vulnerabilities One of the most significant risks associated with APIs is security. Poorly designed or inadequately secured APIs can expose the acquiring company to cybersecurity threats, including data breaches and unauthorized access. APIs often act as gateways to sensitive data, and if not secured well, they can become a weak link. Acquirers must assess the security protocols in place, such as OAuth, token-based authentication, and encryption standards, to ensure the APIs meet strong security requirements. A failure in API security could result in compromised systems, regulatory fines, and reputational damage.

- Integration Complexity While APIs are designed to help with integration, not all APIs are compatible or well-documented. If the target company's APIs are poorly maintained, have limited scalability, or lack proper documentation, the integration process can become significantly more complex. This can lead to longer timelines, increased costs, and delays in realizing expected synergies. It's essential to evaluate the API maturity and development practices of the target company to avoid integration bottlenecks.

- Regulatory and Compliance Challenges APIs that handle sensitive data—such as personal, financial, or healthcare information—must follow regulations like GDPR, HIPAA, or CCPA. Acquiring companies may find themselves liable for compliance failures if the target company's APIs do not meet these standards. This risk is prevalent when APIs are used to transmit or process cross-border data. Failure to meet regulatory standards can result in significant legal and financial consequences.

- Incompatibility with Legacy Systems Many companies still rely on legacy systems that may not be designed to interact with modern API architectures. Integrating these legacy systems with APIs can pose technical challenges and may require more development or re-engineering efforts. This risk can delay the integration process and reduce the efficiency gains that APIs are intended to deliver. Evaluating the compatibility of the target company's APIs with existing systems is key to mitigating this risk.

Opportunities with APIs in M&A

- Accelerated Integration APIs provide a standard interface for connecting disparate systems, enabling faster and more efficient integration post-acquisition. This ability to streamline operations lets acquiring companies achieve synergies quicker, whether it's in data sharing, operational workflows, or extending product functionalities. APIs eliminate the need for extensive reconfigurations, reducing the cost and time typically associated with integrating IT infrastructures.

- New Revenue Streams APIs open up opportunities for new revenue models. APIs can be monetized directly through subscription services, tiered pricing, or usage-based models, letting companies generate continuous income from their API ecosystem. APIs can also facilitate the integration of third-party services, expanding the acquirer's reach into new markets and customer segments. For example, integrating third-party payment processors or logistics services through APIs can create seamless end-to-end solutions for customers, driving revenue growth.

- Ecosystem Expansion One of the biggest advantages of APIs is their ability to foster ecosystem growth. APIs let companies extend their platforms by integrating with third-party developers, partners, and customers. This expansion increases the company's footprint and strengthens its competitive position. Through partnerships enabled by APIs, companies can offer more value to their customers, such as enhanced features, better user experiences, or broader service offerings.

- Enhanced Innovation APIs enable businesses to innovate faster by providing access to new technologies, data, and functionalities without having to build everything in-house. Through API-driven acquisitions, companies can rapidly incorporate advanced technologies such as artificial intelligence, machine learning, or blockchain, letting them stay ahead of competitors. APIs also let companies easily experiment with new products and services, leveraging external data or services to drive product innovation and differentiation.

Due Diligence Considerations in API-Driven M&A

Due diligence is a critical phase in any M&A transaction, and APIs are now a major focus of the technical due diligence process. The success of post-acquisition integration often hinges on how well the APIs of the acquired company will integrate with the acquiring company's infrastructure. A detailed assessment of the target's APIs, their security, scalability, and business model is necessary to avoid future issues and ensure smooth integration.

Key API Due Diligence Considerations

- API Scalability One of the first

considerations in API due diligence is scalability. Can the API infrastructure handle increased demand as the business grows? Does it support high volumes of traffic or large datasets? Scalable APIs make sure the business can expand without significant technical hurdles.

- API Documentation and Usability Good API documentation is critical for seamless integration. Well-documented APIs ensure that the acquiring company's developers can quickly learn, understand, and work with the target company's APIs. APIs with poor or incomplete documentation can slow down the integration process and create technical debt.

- Security and Compliance Security is a major concern in API-driven M&A, particularly as APIs often expose sensitive data and business-critical services. Acquirers must evaluate the security protocols of the target company's APIs, such as authentication (OAuth, JWT) and encryption standards (TLS). Also, compliance with regulations such as GDPR or HIPAA is essential, especially when APIs handle personal data.

- Monetization Potential APIs are increasingly becoming monetization engines for businesses. During due diligence, understanding how the target company monetizes its APIs is important. Does it charge developers for usage, offer tiered pricing, or use APIs to cross-sell and upsell other services? APIs that generate revenue directly or indirectly through partner networks are valuable assets that can enhance the overall valuation of the company.

Valuation Considerations with APIs in M&A

APIs play a critical role in influencing the valuation of an M&A target. Companies with robust API ecosystems are often valued higher because APIs unlock additional revenue streams, enhance scalability, and create new growth opportunities. Valuing APIs, however, requires a deep understanding of how they generate business value, particularly in the context of the API economy.

Monetization Models and Revenue Impact

There are multiple API monetization models that companies may use, including:

- Pay-as-you-go: APIs charge based on usage, letting customers pay for what they use. Examples include AWS and Google Cloud APIs.

- Freemium Models: APIs are free for basic usage but charge for advanced features or higher volumes. Google Maps is a prime example of this.

- Revenue Sharing: Sometimes, APIs generate revenue through partnerships, where the API provider shares in the revenue generated by third-party developers or partners using the API.

APIs that enable subscription-based services or generate recurring revenue streams are usually highly valuable. During valuation, understanding which monetization model the API employs and its scalability is critical in determining the target company's financial impact post-acquisition.

Ecosystem and Network Effects

APIs that connect businesses to large ecosystems, such as developer communities or third-party service providers, increase the target's overall value. These APIs create network effects by enabling more participants to engage with the platform, creating a virtuous cycle where more users drive more value. This effect increases the "stickiness" of the platform, making it harder for competitors to displace it.

For example, Salesforce's API ecosystem lets thousands of developers create applications that enhance the core Salesforce platform. As more businesses adopt these applications, the value of the platform—and the API itself—grows exponentially.

M&A Integration Considerations with APIs

The integration phase of M&A is where most synergies are realized, and APIs are central to making the integration smooth and effective. APIs let companies quickly connect different systems, applications, and data streams, reducing the complexity of integration and speeding up the realization of synergies.

Streamlining Data Integration

APIs enable seamless data integration by providing a standard interface for exchanging data between systems. Instead of having to re-engineer entire data pipelines, companies can use APIs to share real-time data across different platforms, making sure both legacy and modern systems can communicate efficiently.

For example, when an e-commerce company acquires a logistics firm, APIs can be used to integrate the logistics system with the e-commerce platform, allowing real-time updates on delivery status, inventory levels, and order tracking.

Enhancing Product and Service Offerings

APIs provide a pathway for extending the product portfolio of the combined entity. By integrating the acquired company's APIs, the acquirer can offer enhanced features, drive cross-selling, and expand into new markets. APIs also let companies add functionality without requiring deep technical changes, accelerating time-to-market for new services.

For example, a healthcare company acquiring a telemedicine platform could use APIs to integrate telemedicine services into its existing patient care systems, offering a unified experience that includes remote consultations, prescriptions, and medical records.

Building a Unified Ecosystem

Many M&A deals try to build a unified platform or ecosystem that brings together multiple services and products. APIs make this possible by providing the underlying architecture that connects different systems and services. By leveraging APIs, companies can expand their ecosystem and create a more comprehensive offering that attracts new partners, developers, and customers.

For example, when a cloud computing company acquires an IoT platform, APIs let the company integrate the IoT devices with its cloud infrastructure, creating a unified ecosystem where users can manage devices, analyze data, and automate workflows from a single platform.

Concluding Thoughts

"Software is eating the world" and APIs, as connective tissues of the internet have become a driving force in modern M&A. They can enable companies to unlock synergies faster, scale their operations, and create new revenue opportunities. Whether through facilitating seamless integration, enhancing product offerings, or expanding ecosystems, APIs are pivotal in transforming M&A deals into growth engines. From due diligence to post-acquisition integration, APIs offer the flexibility and scalability needed to drive value in today's fast-moving digital economy. As businesses continue to adopt APIs as core components of their strategies, understanding how to leverage APIs effectively in M&A will be important for staying competitive and realizing the full potential of acquisitions

Chapter 10

Understanding Political Risk in M&A

We are living in very interesting times today, the M&A activity over the past two years has been on record high and a very high number of them have been international transactions. In parallel to this unprecedented deal activity runs an era of protectionism, trade wars, currency battles, tariffs and political uncertainty across the world. Many companies have been exposed to political risk and have diluted the value of their M&A transactions. Inadequate understanding of the discipline of M&A due diligence covering political risk has attributed to sub-optimal deal values through M&A or joint ventures.

Challenges with M&A Political Risk

The aspect of political risk in M&A and the associated due diligence is harder to understand because of a few reasons (non-exhaustive list):

- It is a lot more subjective than economic

risk; while economic risk is country's ability to pay back its debt, political risk is the willingness to do so

- It is influenced by law, government leaders, movements, even personalities and their actions

- While political risk needs a framework to understand (focus of this article), it needs deep country level expertise (not the focus of this article) to execute.

- The bias of political analysts that tend to skew towards their areas of interest and subject matter

- There tends to be a lot of information and analysis, but not much when it comes to M&A specific strategic and tactical, execution-oriented advice

- Political analysis is very reactive, and event driven, there is limited ability to predict or generate foresight

In short, political risk is the impact of politics on economic value and markets. Hence basing deal value purely on economic risk can lead to ignoring more serious issues. Some examples are an uncertain Brexit situation, ongoing war in Syria, growing nationalist sentiments towards economics, trade-wars/tariffs, potential slowdown in the BRIC countries, refugee migrations etc. Even if a country's economy is strong, if the political climate is unfriendly (or becomes unfriendly) to outside investors, the risk of diluting M&A value is high.

More savvy investors tend to conduct a political risk due diligence of material M&A deals i.e., not only looking as past construct of events but extrapolating foresight on the future for the acquired business and investment. Early warnings are critical, reading about political risk in the media is often very late to manage the impact.

Political due diligence is not a matter of compliance with corporate governance rules, but a strategic intent to protect the buyer's brand, minimizing economic risk while executing within the environment to create value.

Factors impacting M&A Political Risk

In general, Political M&A risk is equated with countries where there is political violence, movements, frequent changes in government as primary cases. However, M&A deal value can be impacted by several things such as:

- Regulatory changes
- Intellectual Property Laws
- Security Situation
- Legal Frameworks (and ability to enforce laws)
- Accounting Policies
- Society Dynamics

- Business Transparency
- Maturity of Capital Markets
- Interventionist States (many democratic countries have this)
- Military Regimes (running businesses to make $)
- Oligarchs i.e., former businessmen now running states

State authority controlled (or owned) business and their connections (through patronage) or control to management teams can have a different impact from management teams having to build relationships with governments to enhance their business posture or drive government business for their company. The level of these bi-directional relationships needs to be understood and the inherent risks and opportunities in these interaction models should be quantified upfront e.g., corruption levels, decision making velocity etc. E.g., Brazil's government is pressing its agencies as well as citizens to adopt open source software and this could create issues for license and subscription selling software vendors.

Corruption is a key factor which can make or break modern nations, analyzing corruption indices is very important as it can override the opportunities arising from even resource rich countries. For example, Congo is one of the most resource rich countries in the world while Switzerland could rank amongst the least. Their corruption indices are the major difference between how each country has created opportunities for its citizens, businesses, investors and other local and global stakeholders.

Political events are not just about evaluating risks, they open opportunities too. Many political events tend to have some social impact but insignificant business impact, it is therefore important to filter out factors, people and conditions which align with the acquirer's priorities.

The genesis of political risk is usually attributed to countries in transition, off late collision of policies has created a fair share of instability with many regions and countries being directly impacted. In the M&A world, one needs to understand the impact of these policies at an operational level and determine its impact on synergies and future value creation.

A Framework for Understanding Political Risk in M&A

Politics is deeply ingrained in the economic trajectory of a country; the corporate world has not been oblivious to this. Companies with investments in opaque countries like Myanmar or Zimbabwe have understood the art and science behind this. Google, Shell etc. have entire in-house departments dedicated to this discipline. However, it is only now that political due diligence has become important in M&A. It has widespread impact ranging from M&A Strategy, Due Diligence, Valuation and M&A Integration. International markets have become more intertwined than before and a shock felt in one specific country and impact several countries or even entire regions quickly. Perceived opportunities could also turn into risks over a period, for example dependence on China for manufacturing, India for offshoring lower end services or energy dependency from unstable countries like Iran, Venezuela, Russia and Middle East.

Political risk is a function of a nation's stability and can be described as its ability to be resilient to shocks or crisis and its ability to not create shocks impacting the global business and economic environment. The shocks can be internal (protests, demonstrations etc.) or external (protectionism, refugee migrations etc.). Countries like Saudi Arabia are interesting exceptions as they have the uncanny ability to produce shocks at a global scale, but usually tend to ride these shocks because of their deep pockets and authoritarian government. Therefore, the presence of shocks or political fault lines are not exactly symbols of instability.

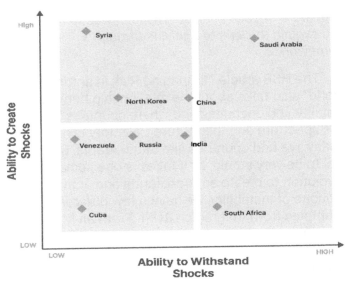

Some countries like North Korea, Cuba etc. are considered stable because they are closed and somewhat predictable. However, when closed countries open, they create massive shock waves of instability, many countries like Soviet Union from the 90s do not make it through while some like South Africa transition reasonably well to stability.

China is a unique exception of being politically closed with a myriad of restrictions on opinion and expression etc., it can be considered stable. But it is economically open, it is a matter of time when there will likely be a single posture for the economic and political landscape. There has been immense speculation on what will ensue after is a topic of immense speculation and debate.

Given the highly subjective nature of political risk, Figure 1 can be debated intensely but it is neither the objective nor intent to depict the exact stability index or posture of each country. The idea was to formulate and explain the lens of analysis through a framework.

The HBR article, "Managing Risk in an Unstable World" also talks about the relationship between stability and openness and where countries lie on this spectrum and their future trajectory is not easy. Today, we find countries like Saudi Arabia, Bahrain etc. to be very stable, all it takes is one social media revolution to create an Arab spring and activate motions of instability, we have a few different examples from that region itself. From an M&A standpoint, key questions are around likelihood of a shock, its timing and magnitude of impact on company priorities and shareholder value.

Operational Considerations and Mitigating Political M&A Risks

One must look at M&A through multiple lenses starring from the M&A strategy itself. A commonly observed challenge is to take an M&A activity based on currency power, on the surface it could look like a bargain but ignoring political risks during M&A evaluation can rapidly derail deal economics.

The operational impact is felt across many areas within a company, it is just not about a legal lens. Political risk can impact sales, marketing, supply chain, production, R&D, Finance, Security, Pricing and Compliance in very different ways depending on the country and nature of the M&A transaction.

Let us understand this through Figure 2

Function	Impact	Key Levers	Examples
Sales	Reduction in volume and velocity of sales	Nationalist sentiments, tariffs, quotas, government policy, regulation	Iraq war created negative sentiment for American and British products in the Middle East
Marketing	Negative brand perception	Job displacement, environmental factors, corruption, inadequate compensation	Amazon and Walmart stalled in India due to perception around job displacements
Operations	Reduced speed to market	Stalled M&A deals, talent recruitment, labor laws, red tape	Increased red tape, bureaucracy, increased compliance costs impede speed of operations is many unstable countries in Africa and Latin America
R&D	IP theft, cost of operations	Weak enforcement, ambiguous laws on IP	Frequent IP leaks in China, spawn local competitors very quickly eroding competitive advantage
Finance	Higher operating costs, increased cost of capital	Unanticipated costs, perception around investment risk	FDI comes at a much higher cost in regions of higher political risk e.g., Pakistan, Afghanistan
Supply Chain	Delays in delivery	Tariffs, trade bans, unions, lack of physical infrastructure, security	Brexit will create additional steps and enhanced process overhead for shipping and delivery of goods between EU and UK
Pricing	Government intervention	Government enforced price locks, tax rates	Government controlled housing in many countries, impact margins of the entire real estate industry value chain
Security	Threats to people and equipment	Non-state actors, history and level of violence, active movements	Terrorism and violence can cause serious disruptions in supply chains
Governance	Reduced transparency and accountability	Poor accounting data, politically motivated hiring	Many military regimes control state run enterprises which are monopolistic, opaque and often critical suppliers in certain given countries

Leading Practices

- Identify and hire a deep country specific political analyst

- Take an integrated view of commercial, operational and political M&A due diligence

- Quantify and decouple economic, political and sovereign risks; translate them into commercial and operational risks and opportunities

- Wargame various high-impact scenarios; develop de-risking plans and model along longer-term horizons

- Assign functional leaders to own, manage, de-risk and execute operational plans

- Reduce subjectivity by creating a range of tactical options, quantity where possible

- Tap intelligence from own company

- Stay informed around critical geopolitical matters in countries of operation

- Anticipate issues, prepare through foresight as insight can go only so far

- Create awareness across all functions and catalog risk and its impact on value creation

Concluding Thoughts

An enterprise-wide response at every single country level is quite difficult, typically a bespoke risk and opportunity model can be deployed given most of the elements are driven by similar societal patterns even if triggers are different. We are the very infancy of this formal discipline in the M&A arena, but given the record deal activity, cross border volumes and increased geopolitical events, it is inevitable that this disciple evolves in a more formal manner and becomes one of the levers of value creation.

Chapter 11

HOSTILE TAKEOVERS: THE DARK SIDE OF M&A

Hostile M&A has been a part of the transaction space for decades. While it gathers much media attention, it is a poorly understood space. Large companies flush with cash will try and take over a promising company to enhance their own position or to simply kill competition. The intent, be it hostile or friendly must create shareholder value ultimately. This chapter will explore several attack and defense strategies deployed during hostile M&A.

In the Mergers & Acquisitions (M&A) terminology, hostile takeover is the acquisition of a Target company by an Acquirer by going directly to the Target company's shareholders against the wishes of their board of directors. Hostile takeovers are generally launched after the formal offer has been rejected, they are applicable to larger public companies for the most part.

There are multiple mechanisms e.g., proxy fights, tender offers etc. Target companies deploy a variety of tactics e.g., poison pills, crown jewel defense etc. to thwart these hostile attempts. We will explore the attacks and defenses in more detail in this chapter.

Professionals e.g., bankers, attorneys, consultants etc. appointed by the target to fend off the hostile takeover through anti-takeover strategy design and execution are called "killer bees".

The Operating Reality

Even a potential threat of a hostile takeover causes the Target's board to deploy "killer bees" and develop antitakeover defenses. However, clarity on who to protect, when and how is a key consideration. Courts typically want to balance shareholder and management interest, but this is not possible all the time and often things skew to protecting management at the expense of shareholders. Shareholders have also pressurized boards of companies like Hewlett-Packard, Bristol-

Myers Squibb etc. to weaken their antitakeover defenses to ensure the balance does not tilt only towards the company management. All publicly traded companies generally deploy at least one anti-takeover mechanism adopting shareholder rights plans.

Attack Vectors in Hostile M&A

There are a few well known attack techniques when it comes to hostile takeovers, typically the Acquirer sends a letter to buy the company at a higher price commonly called a "bear hug". Let us examine a few takeover techniques below:

Dawn Raids

Sudden entry into the stock market by the predator at a price above the prior market level with the objective to acquire a major stake in a very short time – it might lead to a further takeover offer within a few days.

Toehold Acquisition

A purchase of the Target's shares on the open market making the Acquirer a major shareholder and providing an opportunity to sue the Target in case the takeover attempt derails later.

Tender Offer

Premium price offer to Target's shareholders. A tender offer is generally considered a hostile takeover technique; however, it is not hostile if oriented to create shareholder value and such a majority should generally get the deal approved. Tender offers entail a two-trajectory attempt, one front-loaded offer and second intended offer for acquisition. Tender offers are publicly announced, including to the media and SEC.

Creeping Tender Offer

A variant of the tender offer with the Acquirer still wanting to gain majority stake but starts buying stock of the Target at market value until the threshold of control is reached. It is a more gradual process than a tender offer or dawn raid. Creeping tender offers are also cheaper to implement (no premium purchase) and has higher risk of failure if controlling threshold is not reached.

Proxy Fight

The technique solicits shareholder's proxies to vote for insurgent directors on the board or even vote out the current board eventually appointing new management and board favoring the deal. Typically accomplished through approaching shareholders owning large blocks of shares individually. Proxy fights can also increase the number of board members who can sway the voting decisions.

The HP-Compaq deal was valued at $25 Million, yet HP spent significant effort in advertising to sway shareholders.

HP was facing resistance from the founding members and some high-power shareholders who opposed the idea.

51% of shareholders voted in favor of the merger and the deal went ahead as planned even though an attempt was made to stall in on legal grounds.

Figure 5: The Proxy Fight, HP vs Compaq

Designing an Effective Attack Strategy

An effective attack strategy for hostile takeover entails organizing yourself, understanding the Target, evaluating legal pitfalls, preparing the arsenal, disarming defenses, and finally launching the attack using one of the methods mentioned above.

Organize Yourself

One must first ask the most important question if all approaches outside of a costly and time-consuming hostile takeover have been explored and exhausted. Compromises, trade-offs, risks, and opportunities all need to be well understood and clear plans for inability to conduct proper diligence and/or gain Target cooperation must be drafted.

Understand Opponents

Intricate understanding of the Target needs to be mapped e.g., shareholders, management, board members, defense mechanisms, public sentiment, killer bee capabilities etc. This will help inform the time, cost, resources, and attack vector to be deployed.

Evaluate Legal Pitfalls

All other things being in place, a deep understanding of restrictions around legal, regulatory, investment, export, country specific matters must be mapped, and tactical mitigation plans must be created to address items like change of controls, accelerated options etc.

Preparing the Arsenal

The bid arsenal is informed by all the prior stages. It comprises of designing an effective PR/media campaign, mobilizing professionals required i.e., lawyers, consultants etc. and stress testing the timing of the bid. A common practice is to either fully or partially lock-in support agreements as early as possible.

Disarming Defenses

Take steps to maximize shareholder value, tighten arrangements to not violate fiduciary duties of the Target board, wargame tripping of each defense mechanism and create counter strategies. In addition, create anti-dilution provisions and test them.

Finally, pick the right attack strategy and run a wargaming exercise to test all assumptions at play.

Organize Yourself	Understand Opponents	Evaluate Legal Pitfalls	Prepare Bid Arsenal	Disarm Defenses
• Exhaust all option outside of hostile takeover • Define success e.g., board seats, full control, ownership etc. • Analyze trade-offs e.g., red herrings, bargaining chips etc. • De-risk lack of due diligence data.	• Understand target board, management, killer bees etc. • Design target shareholder makeup e.g., institutional, retail, activist, passive etc. • Evaluate White Knights, pill trigger thresholds, possible counter attacks etc. • Analyze defense capability and blueprint scenarios	• Evaluate Antitrust laws, disclosure and other regulatory issues • Understand foreign investments and export restrictions etc. • Evaluate tripping of poison pills, change of control, benefits, accelerated vesting options, coat-tail and "drag-along" rights etc.	• Assemble hostile campaign team(media, consultants, lawyers, accountants, bankers etc.) • Set toehold acquisition strategy (19.9% shares to hedge against superior bid and lower costs) • Lock up support agreements • Ascertain strategic timing	• Device tactical plan to maximize shareholder value • Scrutinize AoI (article of incorporation) to de-stagger or increase board size • Test scenarios e.g., anti-dilution provisions in AoI, beating flip over pill by acquiring control but not executing merger etc. • Launch PR campaign via media

Figure 6:: An Effective Attack Plan

Hostile Takeover Vulnerability Assessment

While a comprehensive vulnerability assessment can be a daunting task, corporate vulnerabilities towards a hostile takeover are also constantly shifting requiring constant analysis. They can largely fall into three areas:

Strategic Attractiveness

A company's strategic attractiveness is dependent on several factors ranging from changing industry dynamics (consolidation), economic cycles, timing, attractiveness of disruptive technology or IP owned, other potential bidders, strategic fit with the Acquirer or weak management teams. There are other factors e.g., limited need for due diligence etc. which can become vulnerabilities. The strategic aspects need to be constantly monitored and understood in the context of the possible hostile approaches.

Valuation Weakness

The lower valuation compared to peers or own history coupled with credit impact, capital structure, weaker management teams and macro-economic conditions can leave the Target vulnerable to hostile takeovers. Other factors such as currency fluctuations, increased supplier risk etc. also cause valuation related vulnerabilities.

Weak Defense Architecture

The obvious aspects of weak defense architecture hinges on the existing shareholder mix, defense mechanisms e.g., change control clauses, shark repellents etc. and inadequate response capability to hostile takeovers leave companies vulnerable to hostile takeovers.

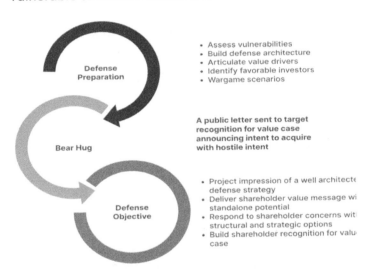

Defense Preparation
- Assess vulnerabilities
- Build defense architecture
- Articulate value drivers
- Identify favorable investors
- Wargame scenarios

Bear Hug
A public letter sent to target recognition for value case announcing intent to acquire with hostile intent

Defense Objective
- Project impression of a well architecte defense strategy
- Deliver shareholder value message wi standalone potential
- Respond to shareholder concerns wit structural and strategic options
- Build shareholder recognition for valu case

Figure 7: Defense Process

Other than the above areas, companies should pay attention to the specific hostile takeover patterns in the market. Many times, these are early warning signs of emerging hostile takeovers. A non-exhaustive list is as follows:

- Massive increase in number of small

stock transactions

- Company executives or board become victims of negative publicity
- Sudden increase from minority shareholders seeking documents
- Other companies have faced hostile bids or dawn raids
- Increase in unsolicited offers to sell shares
- Random rise in inspections seeing customer, creditor, and shareholder information
- Specific activity in activist investor circles, well known Raiders etc.

Hostile Takeover Defense

In general, there are fewer companies which embark on hostile takeover attempts than companies who have been at the receiving end therefore there are more avenues to deploy towards defending against these attempts historically. Defense mechanisms are designed and deployed by organizations through deploying specialist killer bees and tested periodically.

There are multiple kinds of defensive strategies and tactics deployed in tandem or independently, they can be categorized into preventive defense, active defenses, evasive maneuvers, suicidal defenses, and offensive defenses. While each one has varying degrees of risk, impact, and survival odds – organizations deploy a combination of these.

Preventive Defense

Preventive defenses are designed to reduce the likelihood of a financially successful hostile takeover making it more difficult. They are a combination of early warning signs, tight controls or agreements and event-based triggers called poison pills. Let us examine a few of them in a bit more detail to understand them better.

Corporate Charter Amendments

- Deploy staggered board agreements outlining provisions whereby only one third of the board of directors may be elected each year; it requires shareholder approval to implement and classified directors cannot be removed before their term expires.

- Design supermajority provisions requiring at least 80% of voting shareholders approve the takeover, as opposed to a simple 51% majority. This can make hostile takeover an uphill battle for predators.

- Using fair price provision as a weaker defense through a modification of corporations' charter requiring the Acquirer to pay minority shareholders at least a fair market price for the company's stock typically as P/E ratio

Tight Controls

- Use clauses called shark repellants to trigger change control on stock exchanges as a deterrent

- Manage and monitor shareholder mix and trading patterns or anomalies and an early warning sign

- Deploy tighter controls on register and debt

- Design golden parachutes i.e., change of stock ownership triggers benefits for executives

    - Deploy dual cap structure i.e., different voting rights for different types of stock

Poison Pills

These are designed by corporations to poison the deal and discourage hostile Acquirers making its stock less attractive to Acquirers. They were first invented in 1982 to defend El Paso Electric from General American Oil, the first pill was used by Brown Forman against Lenox in 1983. Subsequently, many variants of poison pills have evolved and have been deployed differently. The below table outlines key characteristics, execution conditions and impact of these pills.

Pill Type	Execution and Impact
Flip In	Issue more shares to existing shareholders at a discount when raider attempts to buy a percentage with latter not being eligible for discounts. Could make deal 4-5x more expensive by swallowing the pill.
Flip Over	Allows shareholders to buy raiders shares at discounted price after the deal, owners of common stock receive only one right per share (set expiration date, no voting power). An unwelcome bid triggers rights and trading to trade separately.
Shadow Pill	The pill is not visible or openly advertised, targets could adopt and trigger a pill after the bid.
Bank Mail	Target's bank refuses financing options creating three-pronged impact of increasing transaction costs, imposing financial restrictions and inducing delays to prop up defenses.

Pill Type	Execution and Impact
Voting Plan	Pill is designed to dilute controlling power of acquirer allowing target to issue a dividend of securities with special voting privileges to its shareholders.
Chewable Pill	The pill triggers if minimum price set by the board is not agreed upon leaving acquirer with higher costs of execution.
Dead Hand Pill	Creates continuing board, current target's directors who are the only ones that can redeem the pill once an acquirer threatens to acquire the target.
Backend Plan	Aimed at disarming the two-tiered offer, the pill enables shareholders a right dividend exchangeable for cash or senior securities in equal value to "backend" ask price set up the target board.

Figure 8: Pill Theory

Active Defense

The active defenses are triggered only after the bid has been made. They are more reactive, expensive, and risky. Active defenses also come with higher opportunity costs making it a significant distraction to executives and boards.

Litigation

Initiate court proceedings against the hostile Acquirer stalls the bid, increases bid costs, and buys more time to activate other defenses. Targets must find skeletons in the closet e.g., legal, regulatory or securities laws.

Propaganda

Activate media to trigger public sentiment around opposition rationale, create negativity around takeover tactics, highlight country/region specificity and any grey areas.

Self-Tender

Target purchases paid up shares from other shareholders by sums exceeding share capital to increase the relative voting power of friendly shareholders.

Scorched Earth

Scorched earth is a self-tender offer by the Target burdening itself with debt.

Greenmail

Payment of a substantial premium for large shareholder stock in return for the consent around not initiating a bid for company control. The tax aspects present obstacles for this, statute also warrants shareholder approval to repurchase beyond a certain number of shares.

Standstill Agreement

Standstill agreement is an undertaking by the Acquirer not to acquire any more shares of the Target within certain time. An additional defense usually deployed with Greenmail.

Evasive Maneuvers

The evasion and negotiation techniques are usually applied along with active defenses, some literature even considers it a subset of active defenses. However, they are applied differently and need bidders, allies, and favorable scenarios to play out.   Let us explore the theory of Knights below.

White Squire

A White Squire is a company consenting to purchase a large block of the Target company's stock. White Squires are typically not interested in acquiring management control of the Target but either as an investment or board seats at the Target company.

White Knight

A company which is a more favorable Acquirer compared to the Hostile company (Dark Knight).

Yellow Knight

A company once making a takeover attempt but comes back discussing a merger with the Target company.

Grey Knight

New entrant hostile takeover candidate in addition to the Target firm and first bidder, perceived as more favorable than the black knight (unfriendly bidder), but less favorable than the white knight (friendly bidder).

Lady Macbeth

A corporate-takeover strategy with which a third party poses as a white knight to gain trust, but then turns around and joins with unfriendly bidders.

Microsoft initially presented itself as friendly bidder for Yahoo.

Due to gross undervaluation of their company, Yahoo rejected the bid.

Google and AOL appeared as White Knights to help Yahoo brush off Microsoft, who then threatened to go hostile and become a Black Knight.

News Corp. also expressed interest in Yahoo thereby making it a Grey Knight. AOL later appeared with a proposal for a merger with Yahoo, changing its role to a Yellow Knight.

In the event Google who first appeared as White Knight would gone hostile to counter AOL, they would become the lady Macbeth

Figure 9: Knight Deployment and Battle for Yahoo

Suicidal Defense

These sort of poison pill defenses are used as deterrents but rarely deployed, part of the arsenal but seldom executed given the destruction of value.

People Mail

A blackmail strategy where executives of the Target threaten to resign together in case the Raider takes over the company.

Crown Jewel Defense

A strategy where the Target company sells off its most attractive assets to a friendly third party or spin off the valuable assets in a separate entity reducing interest to the hostile entity

Jonestown Defense

An extreme version of the "poison pill" also called "suicide pill", the Target undertakes activities that might threaten its own existence to fend off the hostile takeover.

Offensive Defense

These are counterattack moves from the Target aimed at the hostile Acquirer to surprise them and thwart their intention.

Pac Man Defense

Based on the game "Pac Man" on the theme "eat or be eaten". It occurs when the Target makes an offer to buy the hostile company in response to hostile bid for the Target.

Fat Man Defense

The Target company acquires a third company to make the hostile Acquirer's bid more expensive

Capital Structure Clog

Target corporation initiates various changes to its capital structure to ward off a hostile bidder e.g., recapitalization, assuming more debt (bonds or bank loans) or by issue of more shares (ESOP, general shares, white squires) or even by buy backs (self-purchase or open market).

Risks with Defenses

While most, if not all defense can counter deals driven by power and greed – they do not necessarily create shareholder value. If outright hostile takeover has grey areas and questionable ethics, so do many of the defenses involved. I have outlined a select few which meet with stronger resistance than the others.

Capital Structure Clog

High leverage can stress the cashflows of the company depriving it of financial resources needed to counter unexpected situations, invest in growth, or return shareholder value.

Supermajority Provisions

Although help in fending off hostile bids, also applies the provision to friendly acquisitions making them difficult, special clauses need to be built to ease this form of defense.

Golden Parachutes

Usually meet with strong shareholder resistance as they get to know this through compensation disclosures.

Pac Man Defense creates no premium to original Target's shareholders; is very expensive and could damage the company, all the premium might go to the original Raider.

Crown Jewel Defense

Might cause courts to disfavor an asset or crown jewel lock up impacting a bidding process

Real-life Examples: Notable Hostile Takeovers

There are many examples of hostile takeovers, in some cases the bids were successful while others were fended off due to good defense strategy and execution. Listed below are some prominent hostile transactions in the history of M&A.

Xerox and HP Inc.

In November 2019, Xerox (a much smaller company) commenced its hostile takeover bid on HP Inc (considered competition). Xerox made its hostile takeover intention public to ascertain their seriousness, HP Inc rejected this offer in March 2020 stating uncertainties and unacceptable conditions. Xerox also stepped back due to the COVID-19 situation; the situation will likely play out sometime in future.

AOL's and Time Warner

Generally considered the poster child of failed M&A from every standpoint. The hostile takeover was consummated in 2000 (valued at $164 billion), but the subsequent dot com and telecom bubble bursting led the company to lose $200 billion in value within 24 months.

Air Products & Chemicals Inc. and Airgas Inc.

The hostile takeover attempt commenced in 2009 and dragged for two years with Air Products & Chemicals finally ending their attempt in 2011. The court upheld Airgas's use of a poison pill, but the onus shifted to Airgas to prove that they were indeed worth the valuation they claimed. Their performance waned during the great recession and came under a lot of media fire. Airgas ultimately exited for 2X the value offered by the hostile bid. Wall Street now holds Airgas as one of the best arguments for management's right to defend its company.

Sanofi Aventis and Genzyme

In 2010, Sanofi's bid for Genzyme turned hostile after the latter's board refused the initial terms. Sanofi tendered > $237 m worth of Genzyme shares resulting in equity ownership of 90%. The deal was eventually consummated in 2011.

KKR and RJR Nabisco

This transaction occurred in 1988 and at the time was the largest hostile takeover bid at $25 billion. The fight was bitter and made media headlines regularly, this was also a leveraged buyout adding to the complexity. With the takeover, the company was saddled with a huge debt load on their balance sheet.

Other notable hostile takeovers in the history of the M&A landscape would be Kraft Foods/Cadbury, InBev/Anheuser-Busch, Icahn Enterprises/Clorox, RBS/ABN Amro amongst others.

There is a new trend with activist investors taking on companies which have been relatively under delivering vis-à-vis peers and there are multiple recent examples of these e.g., Symantec, Citrix, Cognizant, Autodesk, and the likes. They have a slightly different approach towards and more on that later in a separate article. While many acquisitions of Big Tech from the Silicon Valley cannot be categorized as hostile because they are executed in a friendly manner, but the goal is to take out any possible competition leaving limited room for the targets.

Enterprise Defense Architecture

A good defense is built on high valuation, engaged shareholders, an active board with competent management to begin with. However, there are times when things can propel out of sync creating vulnerabilities and distractions. Hostile takeover attacks or defenses are expensive, time consuming, resource intensive and distracting. The art and science with defense are to create more impact or deterrence with limited effort.

A modular defense architecture always helps scale your defenses, one layer at a time. A company should always evaluate the risks, opportunities, and tradeoffs before treading from one layer to the other, as you go up the stack both stakes and risks increase.

Companies also fall prey to the classic dilemma that hostile takeovers are not frequent events and hence not worth investing time or money into robust defense mechanisms. However, hostile takeover defenses cannot be built or strengthened overnight, it is an ongoing process given the dynamic business environment.

	Independence Layer		Stalemate Layer		Deflection Layer		Offence Layer	
	Investors	Growth	Propaganda	Legal	White Squire	White Knight	Pac Man	Crown Jewel
STRATEGY	Incremental shareholder value creating measures	Credible projects on standalone value and growth	Use media, PR and internet	Use breadth of corporate law, actions to protect shareholder value	Replace short-term investors by strategic, long-term ones blocking minority out	Trigger backup plan if giving up independence is inevitable	Propose acquisition of the raider	Propose strategic sale or divestitures of high performing core assets
TACTICS	• Aggressively project long-term play and make equity funding more difficult • Assume more debt to pay dividends. Slowly alter the capital structure but show future potential • Aggressively position long term value creation for shareholders	• Stress on industry dynamics, tailwinds an outperforms rise of peers in the industry • Project growth record potential and performance based on defensible assumptions • Case for standalone value > combined company returns in the long term	• Enhance own image • Highlight takeover tactics • Amplify gray areas in Raider's past or present • Skillfully executive PR campaign to deny public support • Nurture mini campaigns on social media, influence decision makers and shareholders	• Gather and mobilize shareholders • Look for regulations, anti-trust, laws and securities loopholes • Litigate against the Raider using major or minor transgressions or mis-perceptions	• Get minority investment of 4-5% by friendly investors • Tap vendors, suppliers partners to potentially play this role • Adjacent industries, their investors are good sources to consider	• Introduce competitive aggression • Build strong M&A rationale with credible suitor • Identify white Knights who can maximize shareholder value	• Utilize credibility of management and board while projecting superior potential or performance • Assert and position geography, industry attractiveness where possible	• Officially appoint an investment banker to start the process • Leverage board and management networks to explore strategic and financial buyers which increase shareholder value

Figure 10: Defense Architecture Framework

Based on experience, observation, and analysis, I have come up with a framework architecture for defending against hostile takeovers. While this architecture will not fit perfectly to every scenario, most of it works fine and is flexible enough to respond within a process, with the right rigor and structure. I have had the good fortune to implement and test this through wargaming at a few corporations in the United States and Canada, however I believe that these can be adapted to other parts of the world too.

Each layer can be considered a standalone lever to pull or interdependent and incremental steps towards more rigorous defensive positions against hostile takeover intent. As one moves from the independence layer towards the offensive layer the process gets more complicated, expensive and resource consuming.

173

Hostile Takeovers: Ethical Considerations

The hostile M&A actions and consequences have multiple grey areas and require tighter scrutiny with respect to ethics. A few (non-exhaustive list) ethical considerations:

- All forms of suicidal defense result in destruction of shareholder value and are considered unethical

- Fiduciary duties of the Target board must always be respected

- All decisions must be taken in good judgment and only to protect or enhance shareholder value

- Once must abide to all laws and regulations be it corporate, environmental, labor, or international

- The board of directors may not receive any form of payment or unjustified benefits of tangible or intangible monetary value

- The board should not obtain golden shares

Hostile takeovers are here to stay, businesses need to understand the drivers behind them and invest in proactive management of shareholder value, assessing their vulnerabilities and investing in their defense mechanisms. Decimating smaller companies for power, greed and growth will always remain questionable and many corporations will likely succumb to these. Not all hostile takeovers are bad, some of them do return higher shareholder value and it is important to separate the value creating ones from the ones trying to destroy value to satisfy executive egos.

Chapter 12

RETHINKING REVENUE SYNERGIES

Revenue synergies are often considered the most elusive aspect of merger and acquisition transactions. Even disciplined serial acquirers have acknowledged that while they typically meet or exceed cost synergy targets, a much smaller fraction of their deals achieves expected revenue synergies.

The Revenue Synergy Challenge

Senior executives are often reluctant to include aggressive revenue synergies in valuation, typically attributable to low confidence in estimating, capturing, or executing synergies dependent on external/market factors. I have found that developing a standard framework for revenue synergies, grading synergy opportunities, and risk adjusting for uncertain market conditions can lead to quick hits and minimize execution risks. Revenue synergies also depend on variables requiring new skills, methods, products or services, channels, or even a new customer adoption of the product, pricing, and mechanics of the deal itself.

The number of functions involved in delivering a revenue synergy, such as cross-selling of products, is complex and requires involvement from sales, marketing, service, products, customer experience, and pricing, breaking down the conventional logic centered on functional integration and successfully delivering cost synergies.

"Our Corporate development team is very skeptical of revenue synergies. We find it to be an uphill battle to convince the C-suite on any deal centered on revenue synergies."

Senior Vice President, Corporate Development Global Telecom Company

Top Issues With Revenue Synergies

- Actual revenue synergies are often not incremental to the target's standalone plan or the acquirer's run rate

- Commercial due diligence often overestimates the total available market ("TAM") and potential for revenue synergies; speed of execution is not factored in

- Combined products, solutions, and technologies are introduced late or not at all

- Pricing is an afterthought, customers do not adopt and competitors respond with aggressive pricing that catches the acquirer off-guard amid integration efforts

- Execution issues resulting from slower hiring and higher sales attrition prolong the ramp-up phases

- Collaboration within the acquirer on inbound synergies takes a long time to initiate

- Integration Management Office configurations, playbooks, key performance indicators ("KPIs"), metrics, and reporting are all built for consolidation mergers from the 1990s and 2000s and are highly tailored to cost synergy execution

Figure 11: The Revenue Synergy Challenge

Understanding Revenue Levers

Achieving revenue synergies hinges on certain key levers that need to be executed in a specific sequence to minimize risks and maximize value. We categorize them into enabling, alignment, acceleration, and innovation levers.

Enabling Levers

Revenue growth needs a solid platform built on planning a strong integration, avoiding surprises, and laying the foundation for execution by Day One. Typical items of focus for Day One are ensuring talent retention, protection of key intellectual property ("IP"), organization design, stability of information technology systems, and quote-to-cash process. Besides the enabling levers, ongoing efforts need to be applied to the primary levers of revenue generation including brand, channels, products, and customer segments.

Alignment Levers

Acquisitions are rarely done to switch brands — they are mostly undertaken to fill or strengthen capability gaps within existing portfolios. A pervasive brand strategy ensures the company is aligned on this execution. The brand elevation for the combined entity should be the primary goal. Organizations should not get caught up in misguided efforts to preserve the acquired company's brand beyond a certain point.

Such efforts can be a large drain on resources in functions that should drive growth and can also confuse customers. Products and channels must change quickly to fit the brand strategy so it can lay a platform for growth.

Customers are central to any revenue growth strategy, and no organization can achieve revenue synergies without explicitly considering them. Each customer or account lost or diminished makes it that much more difficult to attain revenue synergies. Maintaining transparency with customers, articulating the value proposition early and unambiguously, avoiding overselling, keeping performance high, and integrating customer-related activities while this infrastructure is in place are core elements to the integration strategy.

An important activity that should be undertaken upfront is to design safety nets for customers at flight risk. These are typically customers affected negatively by changes in policies and operational processes or systems that downgrade their experiences with the company. The safety net can be a set of activities that include promotions, targeted incentives, exception management protocols, and executive level coverage.

Incentivizing the sales force to retain customers is also critical to success. A favorable outcome of effective channel integration is to generate a combination of push and pull.

Channels must reach customers in the most efficient and effective way; they can be an integral part of the customer experience. Often in M&A, acquiring new channels and integrating them is a critical goal. Channels need to be in harmony with brands and products. Alignment between sales, marketing, channels, products, and customer segments is the only way to capture revenue synergies. This balance needs to be done as soon as the basic functions and infrastructure are in place and products are rationalized and mapped to the right channels in line with the brand strategy.

Products must fit the overall portfolio and align with the brand strategy because they impact the customer experience; examples of which would include brand names, packaging, and "look and feel." Having a framework to identify, position, integrate, and communicate on products and their value propositions early on is a key to success. Duplicate and competing products must be rationalized, and the sales force must understand the value drivers and the alignment in the new product portfolio. Integrating and mapping the right products to the right channels is vital to realizing cross-selling and up-selling opportunities by hitting the key targeted customer segments.

While alignment is critical, culture should not be underestimated. Culture at a high level can be defined as "the way of doing things." Every M&A transaction and subsequent integration entails a shift in culture, as it needs to be aligned with the vision and goals of the organization and its leadership. M&A executives must recognize the culture needed to drive this shift and must recognize the appropriate organizational design and incentives that will streamline the right behaviors with the desired results. M&A often identifies cultural similarities but overlooks cultural differences, which can make integration efforts more challenging than anticipated.

The key to creating value through revenue synergies lies in the alignment of primary levers. Even when companies do not fully integrate, value can still be achieved by ensuring that the most profitable products reach the right customer segments through the most effective channels, where the brand is already well-positioned. However, misalignment can lead to the opposite result, with lost opportunities and diminished synergies. By focusing on getting the alignment right—ensuring that products, channels, and customers are all in sync—companies can build momentum and unlock significant growth potential.

Acceleration Levers

Accelerating revenue momentum could also be done by leveraging bundled products and services, adjusting pricing to enhance customer penetration or profitability, and implementing sales incentives to drive desired behaviors around cross-selling and up-selling.

Acceleration of revenue should follow alignment — typical successes achieved by pulling these levers are cross-selling products, increased sales coverage, enhanced reach into under-penetrated customers, and new pricing structures that offer more value to customers.

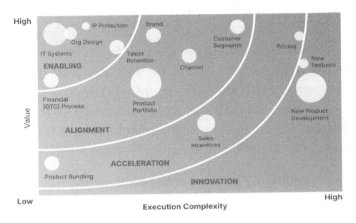

Circle size represents approximate cost to achieve

Figure 12: *Types of Revenue Levers*

Innovation Levers

Given there is new feature development and new product development, developing new avenues of revenue growth by integrating product roadmaps, creating market entry plans, identifying areas of competitive differentiation, and anticipating customer needs and areas of growth are necessary. While new product or feature innovation is on a parallel track, it can be built only on sound execution of the alignment and acceleration layers. The ongoing dialogue and communication channel between product and market-facing teams is important to factor in the voice of the customer.

Concluding Thoughts

While alignment drives 80% of the value, the enabling levers need to provide the right foundation for it, and accelerators must continue the momentum. Innovation levers could cause large leaps to the company's sales trajectory if it is built on sound execution of the other revenue levers.

In addition, the IMO cannot yield optimal results when configured functionally during transactions involving revenue synergies. A cross-functional, value-driver approach is the best direction to take when drawing up and executing revenue synergies.

Chapter 13

REINVENTING THE IMO

As businesses go digital and M&A processes and bodies of knowledge try to catch up, it is also time for the IMO (Integration Management Office) to adapt to the new reality. While valuable in the past, the traditional Integration Management Office (IMO) approach no longer provides the flexibility and adaptability required to manage the complexity and variability of today's M&A integrations.

This chapter introduces a comprehensive approach to reinventing the IMO, focusing on both strategic and tactical configurations. Strategic configurations align the IMO with the unique characteristics of each M&A deal. Tactical configurations determine how the IMO operates in response to varying levels of involvement across different phases and functional areas. Together, these frameworks let the IMO adapt dynamically to the demands of each M&A scenario, ensuring seamless integrations, minimizing risks, and driving long-term value.

Strategic Design of the New Age IMO

M&A deals vary a lot, and so does the integration strategy. M&A integration varies by deal uniqueness, speed, level of digital sophistication, and complexity to execute. For years, IMOs have been one-size-fits-all, with an IMO on the top and many functions executing their integration plans under the IMO. The approach worked for classical consolidation M&A where cost synergies were paramount- these synergies came from a defined set of functions, pulling a specific set of levers. An outdated IMO configuration homogenizes all deal types often leading to inefficiencies and failure to realize synergies.

Given today's business and deal environment, the IMO must be configured strategically based on the specific integration profile. We can define the strategic design of the IMO across four specific axes i.e., deal uniqueness, complexity, speed, and technical sophistication. These axes impact processes, governance, and leadership styles to maximize deal value.

The Four Axes for IMO Design

Deal Uniqueness

Deal uniqueness measures the novelty of the acquisition. Sometimes, two companies may have similar business models, products, and markets, making the M&A integration relatively "vanilla." In other cases, an acquisition may introduce a new business model, product category, or market. These "breakthrough" integrations require a more flexible, agile, and creative approach to manage the inherent uncertainty.

Unique M&A integrations often involve substantial ambiguity, requiring ongoing adaptation and iterative planning or execution. While traditional IMO processes work for vanilla integrations, breakthrough integrations benefit from an agile, experimental approach that accommodates new information as it emerges. The era of consolidation mergers defined the current playbook, but new kinds of deals like adjacencies, acqui-hires, carve-outs, tuck-ins, new business models, acqui-bots, etc. have pressured the limits of the old economy IMO playbook.

Deal Complexity

Complexity refers to the level of operational interdependence between systems, processes, and teams. Integrating two companies that operate with similar business models, operating posture or overlapping product lines may present a low level of complexity, but merging cross-border organizations with entirely different operating models, cultures, and technologies introduces significant complexity.

Highly complex M&A integrations demand robust governance structures, clear communication channels, and a well-coordinated effort across functions. The IMO must set aside substantial resources to ensure alignment and manage the intricate details of the integration, such as data synchronization, process engineering, change management, synergy capture, and cultural integration.

Speed of Integration

Speed is the urgency with which the integration needs to be completed. Some integrations can unfold at a regular pace, allowing for careful planning and phased execution. Others, such as those driven by competitive pressures or regulatory deadlines, must be completed at "blitz" speed, requiring immediate action.

For high-speed integrations, decision-making authority must be decentralized to ensure agility. M&A Integration leaders at various levels must be empowered to make quick decisions without waiting for top-down approval. Failure to move quickly can lead to loss of market share, regulatory penalties, or missed synergies.

Digital Sophistication

Digital sophistication is the degree of technological complexity involved in the M&A integration. Integrating companies using familiar technologies with standardized systems and processes will be relatively straightforward. Integrating companies with cutting-edge technologies, such as artificial intelligence, blockchain, or complex cloud architectures, requires specialized expertise and careful management of technical and operational risks.

The IMO must engage technical or digital experts early in the integration process, particularly when dealing with high-tech companies or when integrating transformational digital technologies. The specialized resources play an important role in ensuring smooth system integration, data migration, and alignment between IT infrastructure and business goals.

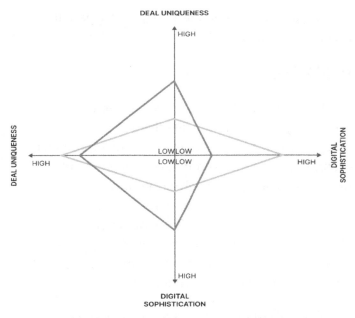

Figure 13: Two Distinct IMO Strategic Design Examples

Adaptive Leadership and Governance

Given the diverse profiles of M&A integrations, the IMO must adopt an adaptive leadership and governance structure that aligns with the specific demands of each deal. It involves configuring the IMO to manage each integration with the proper level of control, oversight, and decision-making authority.

Agile Leadership Structure

The new-age IMO requires an agile leadership structure that adapts based on the complexity, speed, and strategic importance of the integration. For highly complex, blitz speed integrations, leadership must be decentralized, letting teams act autonomously. However, if the complexity is very high and pace is moderate, one adapts a more centralized approach to maintain quality, cost, consistency and ability to regulate speed as needed. For slower, more deliberate integrations, a centralized leadership model with tighter control and oversight may be more appropriate. The centralized control maybe at the IMO, value driver or functional level.

The goal is to balance agility with governance, making sure the M&A integration teams have the flexibility to make decisions while still aligning with the overall strategy and goals of the organization.

Flexible Governance Framework

Traditional governance structures, which rely on rigid milestones and formal approvals, can hinder integration progress, particularly in complex or fast-paced projects. For simple integrations, a lean governance model focused on key performance indicators (KPIs) and high-level oversight may be enough. For more complex integrations, a phased governance approach with stage gates, checkpoints, and risk reviews is necessary to make sure the integration stays on track while maintaining flexibility to address unforeseen challenges.

Tactical Configurations of the IMO

While the strategic design of the IMO aligns with the unique characteristics of each M&A integration, the IMO's tactical configuration determines its specific role and level of involvement throughout the integration process. The IMO may need to take on varying roles based on the complexity, speed, and scope of the integration. There are four key tactical postures that the IMO can assume, depending on the needs of the deal: *Drive and Deliver*, *Lead and Influence*, *Advise and Support*, and *Augment and Report*.

Drive and Deliver

The Drive and Deliver posture is the most active and hands-on role the IMO can take. In this configuration, the IMO assumes full ownership of the integration process, from planning to execution. Workstreams like change management, synergies, KPIs and metrics are owned, driven and delivered by the IMO. This posture is necessary when the integration is highly complex, time-sensitive, or critical to the organization's overall execution of the M&A strategy.

In Drive and Deliver, the IMO manages every aspect of the integration, including coordinating between functional areas, value drivers, overseeing budget and resources, and making sure key milestones, and outcomes are met. This posture is typically required where stakes are high—such as cross-border mergers, major technology integrations, or market-critical acquisitions. Specialized consulting firms are brought in to play this role.

Key Characteristics of Drive and Deliver:

- Full ownership and accountability for the integration.

- Centralized decision-making across all functions and value drivers.

- Suitable for high-complexity or high-speed integrations.

When to Configure:

- High Complexity: When the integration involves multiple systems and functions that must work together in a highly coordinated manner.

- High Execution Speed: When the integration must be completed quickly due to regulatory deadlines, competitive pressures, or risking synergy leaks.

- Critical Strategic Importance: When the M&A integration materially affects the long-term direction of the company.

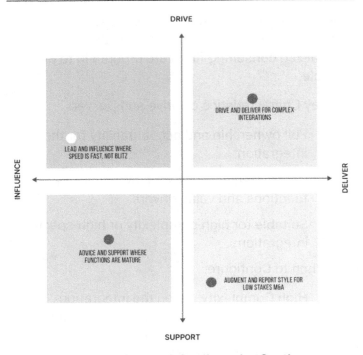

Figure 14: Tactical IMO Configuration Continuum

Lead and Influence

In the Lead and Influence posture, the IMO provides strategic direction and oversight while allowing functional or value-driver workstream leaders to retain control over their respective areas. The IMO maintains governance, reporting, KPIs, etc. synergies are owned and executed by the functions, areas of change impact, and assessed and managed within workstreams (whether functions or value drivers). The IMO works collaboratively with these leaders to ensure alignment between different

194

workstreams and functions, but the execution of day-to-day tasks is left to the individual teams.

This posture is ideal for moderately complex integrations where functional teams can manage their responsibilities but still require guidance from the IMO to make sure synergies are realized, and deal goals are met.

Key Characteristics of Lead and Influence:

- Shared leadership between the IMO and functional leaders.

- Strategic guidance and coordination from the IMO.

- Suitable for cross-functional or moderately complex integrations.

When to Configure:

- Cross-Functional Integration: When multiple teams or departments need to be integrated, functional leaders can manage their domains with IMO oversight.

- Regular Speed: When the integration can continue at a measured pace, but alignment across functions and value drivers is still essential.

- Moderate Complexity: When the integration requires significant oversight but does not need full IMO control.

Advice and Support

In the Advice and Support posture, the IMO acts as a strategic advisor, providing expertise, tools, and resources to functional or value driver teams without directly managing the integration. This posture is suitable for less complex integrations where functional leaders can execute the integration on their own but may need specialized support in certain areas, such as digital integration, risk management, or change management, etc.

Key Characteristics of Advice and Support:

- The IMO plays an advisory role, offering best practices and expertise.
- Functional leaders maintain full control over the integration process.
- Suitable for low-complexity or well-understood integrations.

When to Configure:

- Low Complexity: When the integration involves straightforward systems or processes, and minimal coordination is required.
- Internal Capabilities: When functional teams can manage the integration but need support in specific areas such as digital capability integration, culture, or risk management.

- Knowledge Transfer: When the IMO's primary role is to transfer knowledge and provide the tools needed for successful M&A integration.

Augment and Report

The Augment and Report posture is the least hands-on role for the IMO and many times filled by external resources (more junior folks) from a consulting firm. In this configuration, the IMO primarily provides oversight, tracks progress and makes sure key metrics are tracked and reported to leadership. The IMO does not directly manage the integration but ensures that functional teams stay on track and meet their goals. This posture is typically used for operational or simple integrations where the risk of failure is low, and the primary focus is on efficiency.

Key Characteristics of Augment and Report:

- The IMO provides oversight and reporting but does not intervene in day-to-day management.

- Functional teams, augmented by external resources are fully responsible for executing the integration.

- Suitable for operational or low-risk integrations.

When to Configure:

- Low Complexity, High Stability: When the integration involves straightforward tasks and low risk.

- Mature Teams: When functional teams have well-established processes and systems and need minimal oversight.

- Focus on Reporting: When the primary need is for tracking and reporting progress to ensure accountability.

Best Practices for the New-Age IMO (Integration Management Office)

Align the IMO Structure with Deal Complexity

- Do: Tailor the IMO's structure and governance based on the complexity and type of the integration. For high-complexity deals with multiple systems and functions, adopt a centralized, hands-on approach with clear oversight. For simpler deals, choose a more decentralized structure.

- Don't: Apply a one-size-fits-all IMO approach to every M&A integration. This can lead to inefficiencies and failure to capture synergies, particularly in complex or fast-paced deals.

Empower Decision-Making at the Right Level

- Do: Decentralize decision-making in fast-paced integrations where speed is critical. Empower functional and value driver leaders to make swift decisions without waiting for top-down approval.

- Don't: Rely on centralized decision-making for high-speed integrations. Delays in approvals can lead to missed synergies, regulatory penalties, or loss of market share.

Involve Digital Experts Early for Tech-Heavy Deals

- Do: Engage technical experts early in integrations involving high levels of digital sophistication, such as those involving AI, cloud systems, or advanced automation. Their involvement ensures smooth system integration, data migration, and digital risk management.

- Don't: Underestimate the importance of technical expertise. Leaving technology considerations to later stages can create bottlenecks, data synchronization issues, and costly delays.

Maintain Flexibility in Governance

- Do: Use a flexible governance framework, adjusting it according to the complexity and speed of the integration. For simpler integrations, lean governance focused on KPIs may be enough, while complex deals may require phased governance with checkpoints and risk reviews.

- Don't: Implement rigid governance structures for every deal. Overly formal milestones and approvals can stifle progress, especially in dynamic, fast-moving integrations.

Prioritize Cultural Integration

- Do: Address cultural integration early by recognizing and managing sub-cultures within both the acquiring and target companies. Create tailored cultural alignment strategies that promote cohesion across teams without forcing homogeneity.

- Don't: Ignore the importance of culture in M&A integration. Failing to manage cultural differences can lead to disengagement, reduced productivity, and talent attrition.

Leverage a Phased Integration Approach for Complex Deals

- Do: For highly complex integrations, adopt a phased approach, letting flexibility adapt based on ongoing feedback. Break down the integration into manageable stages and regularly evaluate progress to adjust as needed.

- Don't: Attempt to complete highly complex integrations in one big push. This can overwhelm teams, introduce risks, and result in costly missteps if unforeseen challenges arise.

Use KPIs to Track and Ensure Progress

- Do: Implement clear, measurable KPIs to track the progress of the integration. These KPIs should cover financial, operational, and strategic objectives, providing transparency and accountability for the IMO and functional teams.

- Don't: Rely only on subjective assessments of progress. Without quantifiable metrics, it becomes harder to identify areas where the integration is falling behind or off-track.

Adapt the IMO's Role to the Needs of the Deal

- Do: Adjust the IMO's tactical posture based on the specific requirements of the integration. For highly critical deals, the IMO should adopt a "Drive and Deliver" approach, while for less complex integrations, a lighter touch "Augment and Report" role may be enough.

- Don't: Assign the same level of involvement from the IMO across all deals. Over-committing the IMO to simple integrations can lead to resource waste, while under-involvement in complex deals can cause misalignment and missed opportunities.

Concluding Thoughts

As businesses face increasing complexity and uncertainty in M&A integrations, the traditional IMO must evolve to meet the demands of modern integrations. Strategic designs of an IMO can align its processes, leadership, and governance with the unique characteristics of each M&A Integration. Meanwhile, through tactical configurations, the IMO can adjust its level of involvement based on the specific needs of the deal, making sure it delivers value while maintaining flexibility. A new, reimagined IMO will help companies adapt to the needs of the digital era.

Chapter 14

DEPARTING OLD METHODS OF CULTURE INTEGRATION

In recent years, corporate culture has emerged as one of the most significant challenges in mergers and acquisitions (M&A) integrations. While financial, operational, and legal parts often receive the most attention, cultural integration can determine whether an M&A transaction succeeds or fails. Despite its critical importance, organizations have historically struggled to manage culture during integrations. In the 1980s and 1990s, the prevailing approach was to impose the acquirer's culture on the target. By the early 2000s, the trend shifted toward leaving the target's culture intact. Neither method has proven to be consistently effective across all transactions.

This chapter explores the evolving landscape of M&A culture integration, digging into modern-day approaches that focus on culture alignment over rigid integration. It introduces practical steps and strategies for addressing cultural challenges, fostering collaboration, and building value through thoughtful cultural management. With the right approach, organizations can leverage culture as an asset that enhances business performance rather than letting it become a roadblock.

A Fresh Perspective on Culture in M&A

M&A culture integration should not be about imposing one company's values on another or entirely preserving a target's pre-existing culture. Instead, the goal should be to align cultures in a way that supports business strategy, enhances collaboration, and fosters an environment conducive to performance and innovation. There are also significant differences while addressing culture change in steady state operations versus during M&A as demonstrated in the figure below.

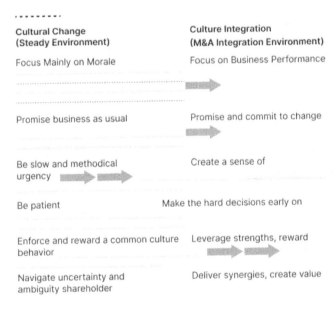

Cultural Change (Steady Environment)	Culture Integration (M&A Integration Environment)
Focus Mainly on Morale	Focus on Business Performance
Promise business as usual	Promise and commit to change
Be slow and methodical urgency	Create a sense of
Be patient	Make the hard decisions early on
Enforce and reward a common culture behavior	Leverage strengths, reward
Navigate uncertainty and ambiguity shareholder	Deliver synergies, create value

Figure 15: Steady State vs M&A Culture Change

Financial Acquirer vs. Cultural Acquirer

In many M&A transactions, the company providing the acquisition capital, or the financial acquirer, is not always the driver of the target culture. Sometimes, acquisitions are motivated precisely by the desire to bring in a new culture, whether it's due to the acquisition of innovative products, breakthrough services, or key industry knowledge. So, while financial synergies might be the main goal, cultural factors often influence the long-term success of the integration.

For example, a technology firm acquiring a startup with an agile, risk-taking culture may find itself torn between trying to have the startup's innovative environment while integrating it into a more process-driven, structured organization. Balancing the desire to maintain the target's creativity with the need to align cultural behaviors is key.

Culture and Business Strategy: A Symbiotic Relationship

Culture and business strategy must be in sync. If an organization's strategy emphasizes innovation, the culture must encourage risk-taking, creativity, and openness to new ideas. But if the business focuses on operational efficiency and process excellence, the culture should reflect discipline, consistency, and attention to detail.

M&A culture integration is not about a quick fix or superficial changes. It requires a strategic, long-term effort to shape and enhance the combined culture in alignment with business goals. Changes should be introduced gradually, using a combination of incentives, processes, and leadership behaviors to pull the right levers at the right time.

Culture Is an Outcome, Not an Input

Culture should be viewed as the outcome of successful M&A integration, not as a prerequisite. Trying to forcibly change culture at the outset often leads to resistance and disruption. Instead, focus on creating a business environment that drives performance, with strong systems, incentives, and leadership behaviors in place. Over time, the desired culture will emerge as a byproduct of these aligned efforts.

Culture Is Not 'Good' or 'Bad'

There is no universal 'good' or 'bad' culture. A culture that encourages entrepreneurial behavior and risk-taking may be highly valued in a technology startup but seen as chaotic or undisciplined in a manufacturing organization. Similarly, a hierarchical, process-driven culture may seem overly rigid to a creative agency but is essential for companies where compliance and quality control are paramount. In an M&A context, the challenge is to identify which aspects of each culture are strengths and how they can be leveraged to improve overall performance.

Sub-Cultures Matter

It is important to recognize the existence of sub-cultures within organizations. These often emerge based on functional roles, geographic regions, or demographics and can be even more pronounced in organizations that have grown through earlier acquisitions. Sub-cultures can either drive positive outcomes or become barriers to integration if not managed carefully. It's crucial to nurture and align sub-cultures within the broader organizational context, focusing on shared goals while maintaining adaptability where needed.

Leadership Sets the Tone

Ultimately, culture reflects leadership. The behaviors, decisions, and attitudes demonstrated by senior leaders shape how the broader organization operates. During M&A integration, cultural differences become more pronounced at higher organizational levels. Leaders must be conscious of their role in shaping culture, aligning their actions and decisions with the integration strategy, and modeling the behaviors they expect from the rest of the organization.

Behavior Change as the Foundation for Culture Integration

Culture change requires behavior change, and behavior change can only be achieved through deliberate, consistent action across multiple dimensions. Six key levers of change—leadership, communication, incentives, processes, decision-making structures, and talent management—must be pulled strategically to influence behavior and drive culture alignment.

Timing and Consistency

One of the most critical aspects of behavior change is timing. The effects of culture levers are not immediate. Leaders must recognize that certain changes, such as new incentives or communication strategies, may take several months to manifest as visible behavioral shifts. Multiple levers also need to be applied simultaneously to make sure consistent messages are reinforced across the organization. For example, if leadership is focusing on improving customer relationships, management incentives and decision-making processes should not be misaligned by continuing to emphasize product innovation over customer satisfaction.

Alignment vs. Integration

Rather than aiming for full cultural integration, organizations are increasingly adopting strategies of cultural alignment. This approach aligns key cultural components that drive value creation without necessarily homogenizing the entire culture. Alignment focuses on creating a common vision, shared values, and collaborative behaviors, while allowing for some differentiation in less critical areas.

Modern Approaches to Culture Integration

Organizations are moving beyond traditional linear approaches to culture integration and experimenting with progressive and unconventional methods that emphasize collaboration, innovation, and adaptability. Below are three modern approaches:

Traditional Linear Approach

In this classical method, the acquiring company typically conducts an upfront culture assessment to document cultural similarities and differences. Leaders then work to integrate the two cultures by preserving the most valuable aspects and changing or eliminating misaligned behaviors. Success depends on leadership commitment, clear communication, and continuous tracking. The IMO plays a critical role in tracking progress and intervening when necessary to correct deviations from the plan.

Progressive, Unconventional Approach

This approach focuses on creating a new cultural identity together rather than assimilating one culture into the other. Leaders from both organizations come together to brainstorm the desired future state of the company, focusing on shared values, collaborative behaviors, and innovative thinking. By involving employees at all levels, this approach fosters ownership and accountability for the new culture. Rather than dwelling on the differences, it focuses on creating a shared future that leverages the strengths of both cultures.

Wargaming

Wargaming is an emerging approach used in high-uncertainty M&A transactions, particularly those with minimal culture due diligence performed upfront. Scenarios are developed to probe strengths, weaknesses, and blind spots in the cultural integration plan. This method tests assumptions and uncovers potential conflicts or cultural barriers, letting the organization develop proactive strategies to address them. Wargaming is particularly useful in transactions driven by revenue synergies, technology integrations, or talent retention, where cultural alignment can make or break the deal. For more details on the Wargaming technique, please refer to Chapter 15 of this book.

Leading Practices for Effective Culture Integration

Culture integration should not be an afterthought but a priority analyzed with the same rigor as financial or operational aspects. Here are some leading practices that drive successful culture integration in M&A:

Rigorous Culture Due Diligence

Thoroughly examine the target company's culture during due diligence. By understanding cultural factors that could affect the transaction's success, organizations can develop proactive strategies to address potential challenges before they become roadblocks. This early investment in cultural due diligence can prevent costly missteps later in the integration process.

Focus on Behavior, Not Just Values

Cultural change is driven by behaviors, not just abstract values. Focus on the specific behaviors that need to be shown by employees and leaders and address them with precision. For example, if collaboration is a key value, clearly define what collaborative behavior looks like and how it will be incentivized. Then, track progress and provide feedback to ensure consistency.

Anticipate Resistance to Change

Resistance to cultural change is inevitable, particularly in organizations with long-established cultures or those undergoing significant disruption. Leaders must anticipate reasons for resistance and address them head-on. This could involve transparent communication, giving employees the tools and resources they need to adapt, and reinforcing the long-term benefits of the change.

Enable and Nurture Sub-Cultures

Sub-cultures can be assets rather than liabilities. Rather than trying to eliminate them, nurture sub-cultures that align with the organization's goals. For example, a product development team with a highly innovative sub-culture can be a driver of creativity, even within a larger, more process-driven organization. Encourage sub-cultures to thrive in ways that support the broader organization's goals.

Language Matters

The language used during integration plays a powerful role in shaping perceptions. Avoid using language that reinforces an "us vs. them" mentality. Terms like "legacy resources" or "target company" can exacerbate divisions. Instead, use language that fosters a sense of unity and shared purpose, shifting the focus to the new, combined organization.

Value-Driven Integration

Align the cultural integration process with the areas of the business that create the most value. Be bold in aligning what is necessary to achieve business goals and remain flexible on non-essentials. Where value can be created through cultural alignment, focus the integration efforts there. At the same time, let non-critical differences coexist, especially among distinct sub-cultures that are not essential to the transaction's success.

213

Concluding Thoughts

Upgrading the traditional M&A culture integration thought process is essential to maximizing the value of any transaction in modern-day M&A. Focusing on alignment rather than rigid integration, organizations can create a cultural environment that supports business strategy, enhances collaboration, and leverages the strengths of both companies. Whether adopting a traditional linear approach, a progressive co-creation model, or an unconventional wargaming strategy, the goal is to create a new, shared culture that drives performance and long-term success.

With the right approach, culture can become an asset in M&A, contributing to faster integration, improved employee engagement, and ultimately, better financial outcomes.

Chapter 15

Rebooting M&A Talent

Introduction

Over the last decade, the business environment has changed drastically, but M&A processes and practices have not kept pace with it. We see several M&A practitioners in-house and consulting firms using the same playbook for M&A Integration from the pre-digital era of the 1990s. Rigid and inflexible M&A playbooks, when coupled with outdated talent, destroy shareholder value rather than create it. M&A deal types, deal volume, and valuations have all gone up, yet the ability to harness optimal value from M&A has been held hostage to dated practices and professionals.

Issues with Legacy Talent

No one can save a bad deal, but outdated M&A talent can make a good deal go bad. While deal-making expertise and due diligence are critical M&A skills, M&A integration is where the rubber hits the road, and value could be created or destroyed. Traditional M&A integration execution relies on the Integration Management Office (IMO), the orchestrator of the execution machine responsible for delivering value drivers. The IMO was once synonymous with M&A integration as a skill; today, it is an essential process or infrastructure to turn the cranks. Value is created through a strategy and operations skillset and IMO is an essential tool for execution. Let us examine a few other drivers exerting pressure on the legacy skillsets.

The Digital Era

Recent advancements in technology, such as artificial intelligence (AI), blockchain, and predictive analytics, have significantly changed the way M&A transactions are carried out. Gone are the days

When traditional IMO and functional project management skills were enough. Today's M&A industry requires a more technologically adept and adaptive M&A talent pool. As businesses increasingly rely on digital infrastructure, integrating technology platforms, data systems, and cybersecurity measures has become critical. This shift has given rise to the need for M&A integration professionals with deep technology and digital transformation expertise. While still valuable, the traditional skill set of IMO and functional project management is not enough without a keen understanding of how to harmonize complex technological ecosystems.

Evolving Deal Types

Many M&A playbooks and skill sets were developed in the past century in the era of consolidation deals, and many companies created science from the art of M&A integration. However, deal variety has expanded, and now we have tuck-ins, acqui-hires, adjacencies, new business models, carve-outs, platform M&A, etc., and the traditional playbooks do not scale across. The nuances range from the design and configuration of an IMO to functions outside the company, deep product integration driving channel revenues, etc. With artificial intelligence and the algorithmic workforce, we will likely see newer deal types adding further pressure on legacy skill sets.

Functional Integration is Old News

An integration management office is the center of gravity during an M&A integration, and its design, configuration, and ability to adapt can make or break deal value. In the pre-digital era, where cost synergies were front and center of value creation, a functional approach was adopted for good reasons, i.e., costs come from specific functions with a few well-defined drivers like headcount, assets, or contracts. They can be executed quickly – hence, it made sense to configure functional work streams. Today, many deals are about revenue synergies, and a single function cannot deliver complete value. The machinery between sales, marketing, service, product, pricing, and customer experience must fire in unison to create meaningful synergies. Hence, IMO needs to be configured by value driver, not by function. Rigid proponents of functional integration will not create value

Industry Skills

In the consolidation era, industry skills mattered little as back-office skills like Finance, HR, IT, Real Estate, Legal, etc., were portable across most sectors and industries. However, the product became the central point of value as the M&A focus shifted from back-office synergies to more revenue synergies. Products across industries are different e.g., the chemical formula of a drug, manufacturing a widget, and building software are different things requiring depth in each area. Given the product is different, they also serve different markets, changing the sales, marketing, product development, pricing, customer experience, etc., around those, making it difficult for a generalist to cut across. This shift has also applied a stress test on consulting firms who bred generalists for efficiency (their utilization, not your business) and now find a lot not marketable to clients. Many are IMO purists or lack the industry depth to harness real value. Synergies come in non-traditional ways today, pushing legacy talent out of their comfort zone.

Functional Integration

Functional Integration
Enhance the organization's ability to compete by aligning and integrating functional assets and capabilities into bundles of competitive advantage through lowering costs and increasing efficiency.

Structural Integration

Enhance the organization's structural advantage (offensive play) or shield the organization (defensive play) from industry structural forces that would kill profit.

Change Management has Changed

During an M&A event, the discipline of change management was considered in the Human Resources or People domain. As the business environment evolved in the prior decade it affected the velocity of business and as a result also responses from customers, partners, and competitors. Managing change external to the organization became equal to or more important than it was internal i.e., people-related matters. In modern-day M&A, change management requires a holistic and cross-functional approach, not a single workstream. Planning, managing, and executing change interventions attributed to brand and pricing changes, competitor response, and product mix requires the discipline to shift from people to market behaviors.

These changes are high stakes and beyond the boundaries of a traditional HR-driven change management skillset.

Change management includes areas like brand, customer behavior, competitor behavior and pricing changes – typically these are outside the realm of an HR skillset

For an M&A integration to succeed, change management must be led by the BU sponsoring the M&A and supported by the M&A integration leader. Change management efforts fail if they are led by the HR silo, alienating customers, partners, and key stakeholders. Visible and impactful internal and external interventions showing a commitment to change must be driven. In the prior decade, many executives promised the status quo to everyone; today, one must stand up and promise change to the market over and above employee communication. Change management is everyone's responsibility, but a partnership between the sponsoring business unit and integration management is the most effective.

Pathways to Talent Upgrade

Rethink Talent Intake

Traditionally, professionals made it into M&A integration with baseline skills around project management, finance, or other back-office functions. As the digital era ushered in, many M&A deals were driven by capability acquisition, new products, channels, or market access. The shift in the acquisition posture required more strategy, operations, and technology skills to get more value out of the deals. Given the lack of skills within existing M&A integration teams, their role shifted to be more and more administrative with time. Old playbooks went stale, and several IMOs were reduced to a reporting function providing status updates for steering committees. This is bad news for acquisitive companies who now need to rethink their talent intake for M&A integration.

Understand New M&A Deal Types

New M&A deal types are emerging due to the dynamic evolution of business landscapes and technological advancements. In response to changing market demands and opportunities, these novel deal types redefine traditional M&A approaches. Platform M&A leverages the prevalence of digital ecosystems, where companies acquire technology platforms to expand their reach and services. Decentralized M&A capitalizes on blockchain's potential, enabling secure and transparent transactions within decentralized networks. Acqui-bots, driven by AI, revolutionize deal-making by automating target identification, due diligence, and negotiations, increasing efficiency and accuracy.

The imperative for sustainability has spurred the growth of eco-friendly M&A, where companies consider environmental and social impact alongside financial gains. As businesses navigate cross-border complexities, regulatory considerations play a pivotal role in shaping global M&A strategies. These emerging deal types exemplify the innovative responses to a rapidly changing business landscape, fostering new avenues for growth, diversification, and competitive edge.

Artificial Intelligence and Analytics

With digital transformation, every business is becoming digital and tech-driven. Embracing AI and analytics, M&A professionals are shifting from traditional skills to more strategic roles. AI-driven insights enable precise target identification, risk evaluation, and synergy forecasting. Automation streamlines due diligence, and collaborative tools simplify integration and improve communication. These advancements boost decision-making, increase deal success rates, and optimize post-merger outcomes. Technologies like blockchain ensure data transparency, which is crucial for compliance, ESG, secure sharing, etc.

From Playbooks to Patterns

Organizations must rethink their deal-making approach. While playbooks offer a structured guide for transactions, they lack adaptability to address each deal's unique aspects. Enhancing playbooks with insights from past M&A patterns can improve decision-making. For example, integrating past challenges into integration planning can preemptively tackle common pitfalls. Standard consulting firm playbooks aren't always scalable or efficient for specific deals. Transitioning from playbooks to patterns represents a strategic shift in M&A, incorporating historical insights. Talent is crucial in this transition, ensuring playbooks stay relevant in a dynamic business landscape.

Make the Talent Decisions Now

In the rapidly changing M&A landscape, organizations must strategically optimize their talent to develop knowledge of emerging concepts, so professionals must be adept at turning technology and business trends into value. The strategic thinkers already transitioned from traditional playbooks to pattern-driven strategies driving holistic value creation. Upskilling is vital for deep functional professionals and functional specialists in areas GTM functions or compliance areas to address broader business implications.

Legacy holdouts like pure IMO skills, and playbook jockeys must be phased out before they erode any further deal value.

Nurturing is essential for digital natives and adaptive change managers. However, those rigidly adhering to outdated M&A playbooks or limited to administrative IMO tasks may not align with the future vision of a company. The success of modern M&A hinges on a balanced approach: valuing knowledge, fostering new talent, continuous upskilling, and taking decisive action on roles that no longer fit. Organizations must make M&A talent rebooting decisions based on value and adaptability.

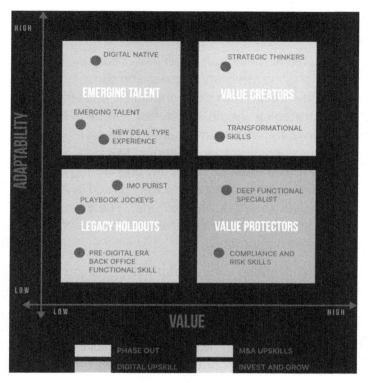

Figure 16: M&A Talent Framework

However, it's crucial to phase out those clinging to outdated playbooks, limited to administrative roles, or failing to recognize the evolving role of IMO. Ultimately, modern M&A success hinges on a balanced approach: valuing seasoned knowledge, fostering emerging talent, continuous upskilling, and decisive action on misaligned roles.

225

Future of M&A Talent

Professionals focused only on traditional administrative integration tasks, and those not updated with modern skills should be phased out. M&A strategies should evolve from process-based playbooks to pattern-driven approaches, emphasizing value over functions. M&A professionals must possess not only strong business acumen but also be well-versed in AI, blockchain, analytics, and, IoT, etc.. The days of just knowing a function don't serve well to support a value-driven approach.

Organizations should prioritize upskilling their integration teams to become value-driven contributors. The future of M&A isn't about adapting but excelling in the digital age by maximizing value. Key traits for modern M&A professionals include embracing change, continuous learning, digital acumen, and adaptability.

Chapter 16

WARGAMING FOR M&A LEADERS

Wargaming for M&A Integration Leaders

"In an era of disruption and uncertainty, developing and executing on M&A planning, execution and integration requires new strategic approaches. Business Wargaming is one such approach, significantly increasing overall M&A effectiveness by providing valuable foresights, stress-testing strategy, and maximizing the potential for successful integration."

- *Nitin Kumar, CMC, CM&AA, CDDP*

Introduction: Hope is Not A Strategy

"One thing a person cannot do, no matter how rigorous his analysis or heroic his *imagination*, is to draw up a list of things that would never occur to him."

A well-worn expression in military circles famously observed by Prussian Field Marshall Helmut von Moltke, and one supported by its absolute truth, is that "no battle plan survives contact with the enemy."

His response to this reality was to have forces under his command participate in wargaming, simulating operational moves and counter- moves on the field of battle in order to surface both unanticipated strengths and weaknesses, but above all, subject existing assumptions to the uncertainties of a fast-evolving, complex situation.

Business Wargaming is an adaptation of this rigorous simulation, but unlike the centuries-old events staged in Prussia, enterprise-level wargames are a relatively recent development. However, their implementation is growing rapidly given the extraordinary levels of uncertainty and disruption in the technology industry today. Said in other words, it is about developing a strategy and execution plan under uncertainty.

Acquisition volumes in both 2016 and 2017 have been at record levels, and as disruptive technologies continue to emerge quickly, we can only expect this trend to continue as the race for assets and capabilities intensifies.

Simultaneously, never have the set of uncertainties dominating the political, economic, and regulatory spheres, the investment community (and the growing cohort of activist shareholders), technology obsolescence and shifting business models - not to mention basic customer preferences - been greater.

In this context, it seems naïve to argue that conventional linear strategies are an optimal way to craft an M&A process, nor will they produce results when it comes to the key driver of fully realizing M&A value: integration.

Business Wargamers can experience firsthand the multiple and cascading pressures from frantic traditional competitors, emerging non- traditional competitors, disruptive technologies, changes in the geo- political landscape and a furious race to acquire digital assets. Acquiring companies can face pre-emptive strikes from competitors on the very targets they had identified as a key pillar of their own strategies.

And, the acquisition itself represents only the very first salvo of battle: once an asset is acquired, executing on all the factors that determine just how smooth and successful an integration will be, in many ways, defines the transaction value far more than the acquisition price.

Organize Yourself >	Understand Opponents >	Evaluate Legal Pitfalls >	Prepare Bid Arsenal >	Disarm Defenses >
• Exhaust all option outside of hostile takeover • Define success e.g., board seats, full control, ownership etc. • Analyze trade-offs e.g., red herrings, bargaining chips etc. • De-risk lack of due diligence data.	• Understand target board, management, killer bees etc. • Design target shareholder makeup e.g., institutional, retail, activist, passive etc. • Evaluate White Knights, pill trigger thresholds, possible counter attacks etc. • Analyze defense capability and blueprint scenarios	• Evaluate Antitrust laws, disclosure and other regulatory issues • Understand foreign investments and export restrictions etc. • Evaluate tripping of poison pills, change of control, benefits, accelerated vesting options, coat-tail and "drag-along" rights etc.	• Assemble hostile campaign team(media, consultants, lawyers, accountants, bankers etc.) • Set toehold acquisition strategy (19.9% shares to hedge against superior bid and lower costs) • Lock up support agreements • Ascertain strategic timing	• Device tactical plan to maximize shareholder value • Scrutinize AoI (article of incorporation) to de-stagger or increase board size • Test scenarios e.g., anti-dilution provisions in AoI, beating flip over pill by acquiring control but not executing merger etc. • Launch PR campaign via media

Higher multiples increase integration pressures and creation of value, and we see evidence of fewer opportunities to achieve conventional back office synergies. This is especially true with smaller digital assets, where the value drivers are centered around products, customers and revenue growth.

For anyone still on the fence, I will argue that the evidence is clear that the time has come for M&A integration leaders to adopt Business Wargaming techniques and practice into their execution strategies for creating value.

Integration leaders need to consider the value of exposing existing strategies – and the assumptions that underpin them – to the fluid, difficult, and fast-evolving environments that any modern enterprise operates in. Doing so means an integration strategy development process with reduced risks due to uncertainties.

In the following pages, I will outline the case for developing a new, non-linear processes that create

M&A value from strategies focused on M&A integration. A key driver of this value – and foundational to testing and refining these strategies – is Wargaming, which develops a framework for strategy through execution based on key criteria enabling optimal integration and value creation outcomes.

Challenges with Conventional M&A Integration

Traditional M&A integration does not typically factor in the impact on deal value due to external factors like competitor moves, customer behavior, in house personalities and other macro-economic forces.

M&A integration creates a highly complex environment with many moving parts: picking the right targets with the best strategic fit, paying the right price and integrating the asset are all essential for creating lasting shareholder value. Typically, a lot of time is spent ascertaining strategic fit through execution of synergies, with limited importance placed on moves or counter-moves by customers, competitors and employees.

A classic example is the Microsoft acquisition of Nokia's handset business, while the thesis was sound at that time and built on the fact that the leading choice in enterprise phones i.e., blackberry was stagnating, and windows mobile could integrate seamlessly into the Microsoft ecosystem in the enterprise i.e., office, exchange, SharePoint etc. and acquiring a handset asset would propel them into a leadership position in the enterprise. It was widely assumed that iOS and Android would remain consumer phones and would never penetrate the enterprise. The assumption went wrong with both iOS and Android rapidly penetrating enterprises at a rate Microsoft could not keep up and derailing the value of the deal. Had these scenarios been wargamed ahead of time, life might have been different during integration.

M&A integration leaders need to anticipate and manage competitor responses or counter-moves to their M&A strategy or integration, such as price drops, enticing customers, PR campaigns, product changes and counter acquisitions. Developing long term integration strategy and sound execution tactics in an era of uncertainty requires sophisticated planning. But planning can only be as sophisticated as the process that guides it, and traditional linear thinking is inherently limited. Wargaming, on the other hand, painfully exposes truth to convention.

> *"The most common issue with M&A integration is that our assumptions around the dynamic market landscape are not stress tested enough for competitor responses."*
>
> *-SVP, Corp Dev & Integration of a Silicon Valley Hardware Company*

Why Wargame? Benefits and Barriers

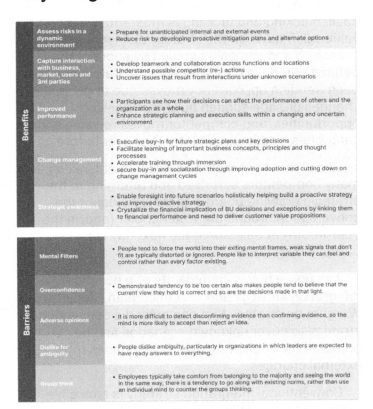

Benefits	Assess risks in a dynamic environment	• Prepare for unanticipated internal and external events • Reduce risk by developing proactive mitigation plans and alternate options
	Capture interaction with business, market, users and 3rd parties	• Develop teamwork and collaboration across functions and locations • Understand possible competitor (re-) actions • Uncover issues that result from interactions under unknown scenarios
	Improved performance	• Participants see how their decisions can affect the performance of others and the organization as a whole • Enhance strategic planning and execution skills within a changing and uncertain environment
	Change management	• Executive buy-in for future strategic plans and key decisions • Facilitate learning of important business concepts, principles and thought processes • Accelerate training through immersion • secure buy-in and socialization through improving adoption and cutting down on change management cycles
	Strategic awareness	• Enable foresight into future scenarios holistically helping build a proactive strategy and improved reactive strategy • Crystallize the financial implication of BU decisions and exceptions by linking them to financial performance and need to deliver customer value propositions
Barriers	Mental Filters	• People tend to force the world into their exiting mental frames, weak signals that don't fit are typically distorted or ignored. People like to interpret variable they can feel and control rather than every factor existing.
	Overconfidence	• Demonstrated tendency to be too certain also makes people tend to believe that the current view they hold is correct and so are the decisions made in that light.
	Adverse opinions	• It is more difficult to detect disconfirming evidence than confirming evidence, so the mind is more likely to accept than reject an idea.
	Dislike for ambiguity	• People dislike ambiguity, particularly in organizations in which leaders are expected to have ready answers to everything.
	Group think	• Employees typically take comfort from belonging to the majority and seeing the world in the same way, there is a tendency to go along with existing norms, rather than use an individual mind to counter the groups thinking.

Figure 17: Benefits and barriers

Companies often have M&A teams focus on the integration process underpinned by the belief that if basic blocking and tackling is masterfully handled, value will follow. On the strategy side, robust searching and screening guided by superior pre-defined criteria is no longer enough. Valuations have been trending up, currency moves due to geopolitical changes provide sudden buying and selling opportunities, and competitor moves re-value entire categories, and happen faster than ever before.

Recall that Microsoft's acquisition of LinkedIn left many competitors surprised and returning to the strategic drawing board – there is no doubt the conversation around the water cooler (and, in the boardroom) at Salesforce the next day was particularly focused.

The figure below, Ingredients of a holistic M&A integration strategy and execution plan, depicts Wargaming strategy that can extend a conventional strategy to cover unknown scenarios and be prepared for counter moves as responses to external changes.

Conventional integration strategy is typically developed by following simple steps based on prior experiences, historic data, industry dynamics and key assumptions projected into the future. This conventional approach only accounts for known business scenarios, can only respond to these knowns and further brings with it historic biases. If imminent variability and uncertainty are not factored into the M&A integration process the strategy becomes inflexible given the rate and direction of business velocity today.

A new approach would need to extend the conventional M&A integration in a manner that factors in counter-moves by employees, customers, shareholders, analysts, competitors, new technologies and regulations. Wargaming – by inserting uncertainty and variability based on a set of immediately relevant factors - creates value during M&A integration if it is embedded in the process alongside the due diligence phase.

Both M&A strategy and integration decisions have huge internal and external impact on organizations. For example, launching an exciting product through a newly acquired channel at the right price might reach more customers and drive sales, but could have difficulty integrating into existing business processes and technology, driving up costs significantly and having a negative impact on profitability. Competitor counter moves that strive to capture market share could further stress the ability to execute.

An example that I have seen over and over is the pricing, pricing is an important lever in creating revenue synergy. Key questions to stress test are what is the right price? What is timing of changes? Should we increase pricing, or should we decrease pricing and drive up volume. How would customers and competitors react to it? A specific technology company reduced prices to drive up volumes and keep competitors out, although it worked in the short term, competitors took that opportunity to reposition their brand as more premium and in the long term gained higher market share with top tier customers.

Wargaming creates a perfect window of opportunity for the M&A integration leaders to look past some of these limitations, align with the changing business environment and prepare optimally to anticipate and address uncertainties.

For a company seeking to understand, say, the risks to a product launch via newly-acquired channels, multiple options and outcomes can be tested through a Wargame style use of existing channels, alternate channels, pricing variability, exploring partnerships and incentivizing customers. The implications of each move, counter moves by competitors, risks and opportunities can be better anticipated, and understood. There are critical decisions underpinning each of these actions, driving a range of possible outcomes. Traditional strategy processes during M&A limit the visibility into uncertainties and alternatives based on moves and counter moves, or even factor personality related surprises, during M&A integration.

> *"A lot of times, M&A integration efforts are slowed or derailed due to personalities involved on either side; planning and factoring these sorts of issues into M&A integration could protect a lot of value."*
>
> *- M&A Integration Leader at a Software Company*

Integration impact variables such as those with high potential towards value of the deal need to be considered into strategy development and execution.

For example, we were contacted by a company where it was assumed after an acquisition deal that 90% of the engineering team would stay on, because the company had retention bonuses in place. The presumption was, of course, that this desired outcome was purely a function of dollars offered. When that assumption did not play out, many integration challenges surfaced and ultimately derailed the value of the entire transaction to irrecoverable levels.

There are no uncritical loyalties in business, however, and so a Business Wargamer would have asked – early on – what if the core team doesn't stay?

Design Considerations for Wargames (or, When to Play?)

Wargames can help enable foresight into future scenarios to build a proactive strategy and improve existing reactive strategies.

A Wargame is best suited to deals with a moderate level of uncertainty. Extremely high levels of macro uncertainty (like the impact of nanotechnology on the design of next generation products, for instance) will understandably make it hard for any strategist to plot a range of defined outcomes.

Wargames are best used under conditions where two or three results seem viable alongside each strategic option. In these scenarios analysis tends to be complex, while yielding limited results. Wargames bring forth the range of options available to executives for strategic decision making and execution tactics.

The narrower the options and uncertainty, the more successful the Wargame is since we know the game and must play to win it.

On the other hand, if the degree of uncertainty is too high and the options are several or, even, infinite, we must first engage in scenario planning to define the game. These situations are not suited to deploy winning Wargames.

The area in between the two spectrums of uncertainty would entail strategy workshops to plot the trajectory of moves and to narrow the options from several choices to a group of finite choices. You now know what the game is, but still must define where to play it. This would still be out of reach from the Wargaming sweet spot.

Once the decision to deploy Wargaming is made, the next decision is to determine the kind of Wargame to deploy.

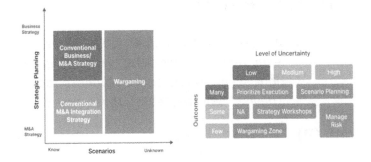

Figure 18: Where to Deploy Wargames

Wargaming Playbook: Unpacked

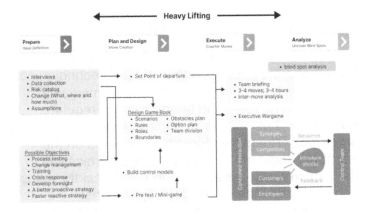

Professionals e.g., bankers, attorneys, consultants etc. appointed by the target to fend off the hostile takeover through anti-takeover strategy design and execution are called "killer bees".

Types of Wargames

> *Wargames are dimensioned by types and level; deploying the right wargame in the right scenario is a critical success factor. The list below addresses these examples.*

Path (P)

Path Wargames consider all the merging organizations' resources and focus on a long term roadmap (3-5 year) along all possible dimensions. The focus is not on any one issue but on a broad range of business implications based on M&A strategy and integration decisions. Individual issues may not be represented in isolation.

This simulation considers macroeconomic factors like the political, economic and technological impacts on the integration. This assessment will involve several roles and teams such as regulators, R&D teams, businesses, multiple competitors, strategic partners, vendors etc.s. Focus is on the economic logic of the industry, the dynamics within the industry, any possible technology breakthroughs and cost management through operational excellence. Selecting and stress testing the right procurement process and validating if it truly adds synergy would be an example of a path wargame. The comprehensive strategy of an organization based on M&A strategy, valuation or integration is an example of a path wargame.

Grand Strategy (GS)

The Grand Strategy Wargame focuses on the possible outcome(s) of the overall M&A strategy, due diligence, valuation and integration planning. The timeframe is usually considered the end of the integration effort and any moves by key players help uncover unknowns. Ranges of multi-dimensional and cross functional outcomes are considered, and competitor moves are usually a vital success factor in this sort of Wargame.

Landscape (L)

Landscape Wargames are designed to consider changes in the operating landscape such as industry consolidations, competitor M&A, emerging business models, serial M&A activity or a new regulatory change. These wargames also help Integration teams prepare for various outcomes, launch and integrate new and improved products, replace and retire end of life products and decide how much effort should ultimately be invested. These games are geared towards adapting to the new business landscape.

Test (T)

This Wargame tests an already developed strategy against surprises and uncertainties stemming from competitor responses, business changes and unplanned moves from customers, channel partners, government, regulators and vendors bringing in breakthrough products and technologies. The Test Wargame is often the most popular, because the timeline of decisions in most companies is more suited to building a strategy at a product, business unit or regional level, and then testing it upfront. A good example of this game is testing the implications of a new change due to a single integration decision that impacts the business.

Wargame levels

In addition to picking the right situation, it is also important to determine the right level for the game. While working with M&A Leaders, exercises can be conducted at four increasing intensity levels.

Level I

Level I is the simplest level of Wargame and usually involves tackling one scenario based on a specific situation or decision. This level is usually undertaken when there is a significant level of change being introduced and multiple outcomes are possible. A typical example of a Level I Wargame would be a new process or change to an existing process that has multiple potential results affecting more than one group of stakeholders.

Level II

Often designed to serve as a "consciousness raiser," Level II helps participants understand key issues and concerns related to their own organization and capabilities. The Wargame is customized to reflect an organization's specific strengths, technology landscape, business model alignment and competitors, and involves multiple sessions across a couple of days. An example of a Level II Wargame would be selecting Enterprise Resource Planning (ERP) packages from one of two vendors, a decision that will have a widespread technological impact on internal and external stakeholders.

Level III

Level III is more intensive and aimed at helping develop and/or evaluating strategies to deal with a multitude of issues occurring in tandem. It involves the preparation of a significant amount of background material and extensive customization to reflect the real personnel, skills, products, competitors, vendors and uncontrollable factors as much as possible. Level III Wargames could easily last a few weeks and encompass multiple moves. For example, a decision to pick one target over another in single or multiple geographic locations has a significant impact on supply chains, tax rates, hard costs, employee locations, products, customer segments, competitive landscape and geography specific regulations, all of which need to be considered.

Level IV

The most intensive level of M&A Wargaming is Level IV which often involves two or more separate sessions, each two to four days in duration. This level is usually designed to help conduct a very detailed evaluation of the integration strategy's impact on the organizational strategies and supporting operational level tactical plans before a company makes a final commitment to implement them. It is commonly used in large scale, complex and multi-geographical deals, and can be used extensively under divestiture or carve out scenarios and played in the PATH game configuration.

Based on the company and integration needs, a framework can be used to help M&A leaders pick the right type and level of Wargaming. Various scenarios can be mapped onto this framework to determine the level of effort and depth required. A sample illustration is depicted in the figure below. While every situation may not precisely fit, approximations with tweaks are often effective. These frameworks are also dependent on the industry, organization size, industry dynamics and the current state of the business.

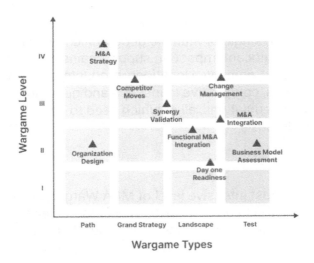

Figure 19: Examples of wargaming types and levels

Potential M&A Integration Wargaming Scenarios

Wargames can be deployed to develop better foresight across several areas of M&A Integration, creating, capturing and protecting value.

Wargaming can be used as a key M&A integration capability enhancement tool by M&A Leaders in multiple scenarios as it enables foresight into external and internal actions and reactions to the strategy from the industry, market and/or internal organizational units. Depending on the maturity of the integration, an appropriate Wargame type and level can be chosen and conducted as described in the previous chapter, whether the company is initiating a formal integration for the first time, conducting an outcome assessment exercise or evaluating the current integration strategy based on a specific situation.

The following are some of the sample scenarios where Wargaming could be efficiently used to enable foresight. These scenarios can significantly impact the business on an individual basis or as a combination.

Landscape Evaluation

In today's world, acquisition volumes are high and companies are racing to gain access to new and unique capabilities, customers and emerging technologies. The target universe is limited, forcing higher valuations and competition among acquirers. Most companies want to build a grand strategy for M&A to understand how the ecosystem around them will evolve and respond. For example, what is the implication to Salesforce of Microsoft acquiring LinkedIn? How should Salesforce respond? Where will Microsoft and Oracle make their next acquisition? What is the integration strategy and execution approach underpinning each acquisition?

Develop foresight

M&A integration situations create flux due to the dynamic and complex business environment. Developing foresight is not easy when every decision has multiple outcomes, risks and opportunities. Wargaming can help bring clear buying possibilities and integration strategies to the fore. Competitor reactions to the deal, value paid and possible value created are all critical inputs to integration teams, who must now execute testing several scenarios against anticipated issues.

M&A Integration Governance

Selecting the right governance model for integration is critical to maximize deal value. In the old world, M&A integration leaders used a single model which comprised of leaders and executives from the two companies and constituted a steering committee. The composition of the steering committee was largely based on where the most influential executives were located, and the deal sponsor largely made the decision. Today, governance models need tightly align with the nature of the deal, and there are a variety of models to choose from: centralized, decentralized, top down (management centric), bottom up (customer centric) and others. Wargaming helps integration governance pick the right model for the right type of deal to maximize decision making, speed of execution, drive accountability and to ensure maximum shareholder value.

Integration Management

Managing the integration requires a dedicated Integration Management Office (IMO). If one compares the governance to, say, air traffic control, the IMO is tasked with actually flying the plane – safe takeoff and landing is critical for protecting and creating value. Management needs to understand the implications of having functional versus cross functional IMOs and its impact on synergies and value. In addition, there are several configurations for IMO deployment and their posture can vary depending on the deal size, complexity and metrics. IMOs can assume a "drive and deliver" posture or a "lead and influence" posture to create value. Wargaming can ensure the IMO has the right level of leeway to deliver optimal results.

Day One Planning And Execution

Transition into day one with no surprises, in a smooth manner, is crucial and many variable and moving parts have to be managed in conjunction with several risks and interdependencies. Poor execution, uncertainty and surprises can lead to issues around brand image, customer retention, channel conflicts, employee anxiety, productivity dips, service disruption and flight of talent. Wargaming can help proactively anticipate these issues and decision impact, while mitigating risks – it can also simplify change buy-in from executives and employees and inform organization design, go to market strategies and other initiatives.

Synergies

The synergies that were modeled during the due diligence need to ultimately be validated and realized. There are many business and execution risks to be anticipated and managed, and many times there are unanticipated issues creating bottlenecks that either leave synergies unrealized or delay time to realized shareholder value. Categorizing synergies and understanding the risks to the execution are important, and simulating the key value drivers around cost and revenue synergies along with associated dependencies is a key role for Wargames.

The "How Much" Decisions

Several situations arise when executives think about how much time, energy, resources, efforts and money are necessary to make the integration successful. Special situations or integration patterns that have never been undertaken before have no precedent or experience to inform decion-makers. Integrating too quickly and too much can have consequences, and so can integrating very slowly and in a limited way. To get an estimate around the same, it is advised that M&A integration teams conduct small-scale war games to arrive at the right range and figure out "how much."

Customer Impact

Customers are the heart and soul of any M&A and impacting customers negatively can destroy deal value. Wargaming not only helps protect value through well informed reactive strategies but can also proactively resolve key customer-facing issues such as brand alignment, channels, key customer segments, products and momentum acceleration by better aligning pricing and incentives. It helps companies understand potential competitor moves, customer reactions, product launches and time to value.

Human Capital Impact

Wargaming helps inform organization design, proactively address employee morale and anticipate risk factors towards flight of key personnel. It is also a tool to gain buy-in from employees and engage them in the M&A integration effort, compelling them to understand problems and solve them. It is also typically used in situations where change management is required, or choices are made about systems selection, operational policies and pricing. Additionally, the personality factor can never be ignored during M&A integration, like decision making, leadership styles, communication styles and their impact on the integration roadmap and deal value.

Execution of M&A Wargames

It's time to play!

The practical execution of an M&A Wargame depends on the complexity of issues to be addressed, the level at which it is conducted, and the number of stakeholders involved. The figure below depicts a self-explanatory and generic framework which could be used to conduct a four-phase Wargame.

M&A wargames typically have four or more teams: the home team, the control team, the business team, competitors and employees.

An important aspect of successfully conducting a Wargame is to identify a control team which plays a key role in designing the Wargame by selecting the right type and level. This team can be from within the organization, or consultants who have extensive experience conducting Wargames and are viewed as neutral coordinators. This team focuses on keeping the game on track, introducing uncertainties, changing the game dynamics and representing any entities that have not received adequate representation such as the regulators, customers or government officials.

The control team coordinates with the teams separately to plan various moves and counter-moves, keeping teams and discussions in isolation to avoid decisions being influenced prior to the actual Wargame. The execution is an iterative process and can be planned across one to five sessions based on the complexity and levels. It is important that de- briefs are conducted and factored into the game for subsequent sessions so that outcomes accurately represent incremental learning from rounds.

Each round comprises at least one strategic move; normally Wargames are designed for at least three strategic moves across any given timeframe.

Home Team

The home team comprises the M&A leader(s), organization executives and key functional leaders who make the strategy and integration decisions in line with the integration strategy. This team will anticipate counter moves from the other constituents.

Competitor Team

The competitor team will respond to any opportunities arising from the uncertainty created during strategy or integration, and will make countermoves including attracting key talent, customers and taking advantage of any other strategic lapses from the home team.

Customer Team

The customer team comprises a well-planned mix of the most loyal, fringe and opportunity based customer segments that would each react differently – and potentially in opposition with one another - to moves from home and competitor teams. If need be, more than one customer team can be brought into the mix based on size and complexity of each customer segment.

Employee Team

It is important to assess, factor and manage the employee impact and flight risk. This team is critical to assess the execution capacity of the organization, as well as engage and proactively build a retention strategy for talent.

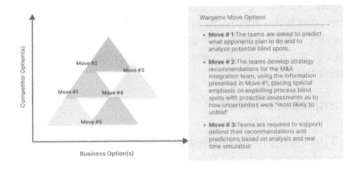

Benefits and Use Cases

Picking the right scenario and Wargame allows for any given timeframe.

The right people, levels and ingredients introduced into a Wargame bring several advantages. The involvement of select board members, executives and line managers in the exercise who "live" the strategy and the consequences of the decisions improve Wargame effectiveness.

Wargaming also makes learning from mistakes easier; it tests reactions to different situations and brings the capabilities of the organization to the surface. Another advantage is that radical moves are possible, challenging all assumptions, uncovering blind spots and stress testing the economic logic under specific acquisitions or business models.

Simulating competitor moves brings forth innovative approaches previously not considered. Below are some very specific benefits of applying Wargaming to M&A Integration scenarios.

Common Pitfalls and Best Practices

Although every situation is unique and there is no 'one size fits all' approach when it comes to Wargame design for M&A, there are certain practices which, when followed, will enhance success. Common considerations are outlined below:

- Identify and pick the right situations to use Wargames i.e., low to moderate uncertainty, outcomes should be limited range of options rather than infinite

- The right level and type of Wargame must be identified; A corresponding number of moves must be designed.

- Involve the right roles and invite the right people from the organization; limited stakeholders bearing quantifiable impact through each other's decisions and actions

- Automated software cannot (yet) replace human intelligence, decision-making and intuition, avoid automated games (after all, in the real world, you're still competing with people and not AI)

- Over-engineering problems do not help the cause, keep issues close to reality (planning for the Zombie Apocalypse, for example, is arguably unnecessary)

- Best Practices for enterprise Wargaming are as follows:

- Keep the games and moves simple, complicated games will divert energy on non-essential items

- All roles and players need to have meaningful dynamics between them to generate the right counter moves

- Give yourself time: do not run the Wargame very close to the D-day, it might not yield desired results and in fact be counterproductive by distracting from the actual event itself

- Empowerment to ask questions and challenge assumptions is crucial: if an organization's management and culture do not support challenging existing thinking, then stay away from Wargames

- Assess competitive blind spots as they arise – understand where you need additional focus and insights

- Challenge all assumptions, think like competitors and challenge the boundaries

A Case Study

A technology company announced the acquisition part of their strategy to pivot their business model and enhance their competitive advantage through a new acquisition. The Acquirer had never run the business model that Target company delivering to customers although the products solved the same problem. There was a large premium paid for the acquisition and the deal thesis was heavily counting on delivery of revenue synergies, given the risk of one business model cannibalizing the other – executives and M&A integration leaders decided to embark on a Wargame to develop foresight

As a concept Wargaming has been around for more than a century; in the recent past it has gained acceptance amongst business and M&A leaders when it comes to strategy development and strategy testing.

It is still in its infancy of application during M&A integration scenarios but is fast catching up in more complex deals and environments.

The truth is that M&A strategies cannot be built in a vacuum; they need to align with the business environment and the operating model. At the same time, simply "hoping" an M&A acquisition and integration strategy will work is hardly a productive way to operate in the current environment.

Dozens of uncontrollable uncertainties exist after a deal is announced, and every subsequent decision has a high impact on the business (and its value), be it managing change or protecting brand reputation.

Exposing a strategy and tactics to the clarity – and potentially difficult truths - provided via Business Wargaming radically transforms a company's odds when facing marketplace uncertainties, and it is our belief that early adopters of the practice will significantly outperform their competitors.

Epilogue

Technology continuously reshapes landscapes and redraws boundaries, the field of mergers and acquisitions (M&A) stands at a pivotal juncture. The convergence of software as a service (SaaS), blockchain, artificial intelligence (AI), and the Internet of Things (IoT) has not merely altered the playing field; it has introduced a new game with its own set of rules. This book serves as your compass in navigating this uncharted territory, ensuring you not only keep pace with the digital revolution but also lead the charge in transforming M&A practices.

The real-world applications of the strategies discussed herein are both vast and varied. From enhancing due diligence processes with AI to leveraging blockchain for more secure and transparent transactions, these technological advancements offer practical solutions to age-old M&A challenges. By adopting these strategies, you can significantly reduce risks, uncover hidden value, and create synergies that propel your deals towards unprecedented success.

We've journeyed through the intricacies of digital transformation in M&A, **highlighting key areas** such as deal sourcing, valuation, due diligence, and integration. The essence of our discussions underscores a singular truth: mastering these new technologies is not an option but a necessity for anyone aspiring to excel in today's M&A landscape.

To **put what you've learned into action**, start small but think big. Identify one or two areas within your current M&A practice where integrating technology could yield immediate benefits. Whether it's employing AI algorithms to analyze potential deal synergies or using IoT data to gain deeper operational insights during due diligence, each step forward is a leap toward mastering digital-age M&As.

While this book aims to equip you with the knowledge and tools necessary for thriving in digital M&A, it is by no means exhaustive. The rapid pace at which technology evolves demands continuous learning and adaptation. As such, I encourage further exploration and experimentation within your organizations and industries.

As we close this chapter (and indeed this book), let us not view it as an end but as a beginning—the start of a transformative journey in your professional life. Armed with the insights from these pages, you are now better positioned to navigate the complexities of modern M&As with confidence and acumen.

Let this book be both your inspiration and your guide as you reinvent yourself and your approach to digital M&A.

Call to Action

Can I ask a Favor?

If you enjoyed this book, found it useful, or otherwise please post a short review on Amazon. Please share this with others who may find it valuable too.

I read all the reviews personally so I can continually write what people want.

Thanks for your support!

ABOUT THE AUTHOR

Nitin Kumar is a two-decade veteran in the Hi-Tech industry, he serves on boards and is a well-established CEO having led multiple global companies.

In his prior career as a Management Consulting Partner, he served many Corporate and Private Equity clients. Nitin has added value to over 1000 M&A deals spanning Consolidation Plays, Adjacency Moves, Technology Tuck-ins, New Business Model Transition, Distressed M&A, Acqui-hires, Hostile Takeovers, and Activist Offense/Defense. He has also led high-profile and complex divestitures.

He has won several international awards for pioneering new approaches in the M&A discipline and is considered one of the leading global thought leaders in this discipline.

Nitin is a Certified M&A Advisor, a Chartered M&A Professional, a Certified Post Merger Integration Professional, a Certified M&A Specialist, and a Certified Due Diligence Professional.

THANK YOU